The Road to India

GUIDE TO THE OVERLAND ROUTES
TO THE EAST

John Prendergast

JOHN MURRAY · LONDON

© John Prendergast 1977

All rights reserved. No part of this
publication may be reproduced, stored in
a retrieval system, or transmitted, in any
form or by any means, electronic, mechanical,
photocopying, recording or otherwise,
without the prior permission of
John Murray (Publishers) Ltd.,
50 Albemarle Street, London, w1x 4bd

Printed in Great Britain by
Cox & Wyman Ltd
London, Fakenham and Reading
0 7195 3396 1

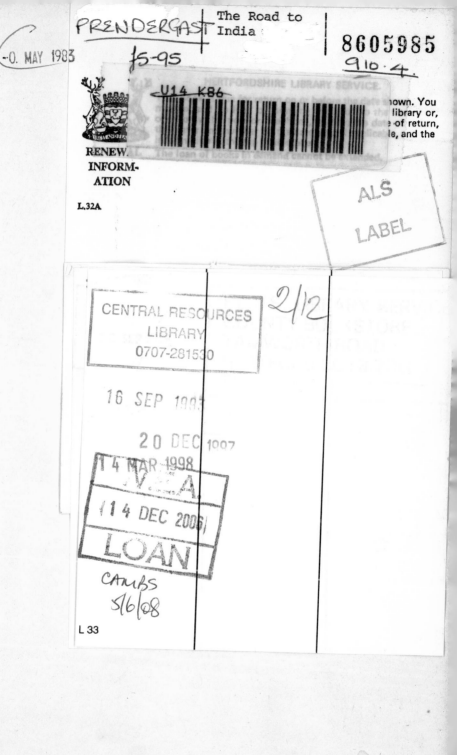

THE ROAD TO INDIA

To my Wife and Navigator

Contents

Acknowledgements

My deepest thanks are due to all our friends in India and Pakistan for their kindness during our many journeys: particularly Colonel Kush Wakht Ul Mulk and Anne Ransome, MBE in Pakistan, Bill and Lyn Grimsley of the U.S. Embassy in New Delhi for their great hospitality when we have been in that city, and the U.P. Forestry Dept whose members have helped to make Corbett National Wild Life Park almost a second home for us. Apart from giving us the pleasure of their company in the Park, Edmund Makrill, Peter Childs and John Walker very kindly checked our experiences on the southern route through Iran and brought them up to date as well as surveying the alternative round the Tahir Pass in Turkey through Kars. My deepest thanks also to Brigadier V. Wainwright, OBE, MC, for providing the Turkish phrases and to my editor, Roger Hudson of Messrs John Murray, for his advice in the preparation of the book.

Conditions on the overland route are always changing and John Murray would appreciate having any inaccuracies pointed out. Please write to 50 Albemarle Street, London, W1X 4BD.

Part One

Part One

1. *Introductory*

I have written this book as an ordinary man for ordinary men about an activity a little out of the ordinary. I refer to driving overland to distant countries. I have taken the run from England to India, with variations, as my yardstick. This is because the route goes through areas of extreme climate and altitude, whose grandeur of scenery is hard to match. I say yardstick because the lessons learnt this way will stand you in good stead on other lofty motor journeys in most parts of the world.

More than on any other route, you travel through areas of the greatest historical interest for our civilization. You can for example see the foundations of the earliest cities, Hellenic remains, parts of Alexander's route to India and the relics of the Byzantine, Seljuk, Ottoman and Persian Empires. To cap it all India, the most kaleidoscopic of countries, awaits you. If you are thinking of going on afterwards to Singapore, Malaysia or Australia I have covered the route within India down to Madras which is the accepted port for transhipment farther east.

I think I can say that I am an ordinary person as I'm not a particularly good mechanic or very practical. What I have got to offer however, are commonsense ideas based on a great weight of experience. With their help you will be able to avoid a lot of the potholes into which I have fallen. I have served for years in India, what is now Pakistan, and Afghanistan and have visited them again frequently in recent years, as well as motoring extensively in Iran and Turkey. I used to spend holidays in Kashmir up to 1947 and have renewed my acquaintance since. I am qualified in languages – Urdu/Hindi, Pushtu, Persian – all relevant to the journey, but by no means essential. In all I have done the return overland journey to India eight times since retirement, the last trip recently, and have stayed in India for four to five months each year. I think I have chosen the best main route. It may not always agree with those preferred in other guide books, but then these are often based on information from local tourist associations who tend to describe a route as it is eventually intended to be, but not as it is at present.

Motor-caravanning is not cheap under any circumstances, though for a large stretch of the route fuel is cheaper than in Europe. The cheapest way of getting to India must be a charter flight or one of the numerous bus packages now available. On the other hand my method is not 'big time' like blue sea yacht cruising, for which you need specialized knowledge and a great deal more money. Remember that you will have your accommodation and transport with you when you get to your destination. In India for instance, any hotel that is not pretty fly-blown is as expensive as in England. Although public transport is cheaper, it requires enormous stamina as well as endless patience and a good pair of elbows, to use it.

You do not need any special qualifications for the India run. All can go, from pensioners to young children, provided they take their parents with them. It can be just a pleasant long drive with only minor checks and trials, but you must follow certain principles, chief among which is to travel at the optimum seasons of spring and autumn.

In the last two chapters of the book I have included details of a number of side trips or alternative routes in Pakistan, Iran and Turkey. If you have the time and money to be able to take your eye off the main target (India on the way out, Europe on the way back), then you will get enormous pleasure from, for example, visiting Isfahan, the Black Sea, or the southern coast of Turkey.

I have driven two diesel vehicles and one petrol vehicle. I have tried the stock-in-trade camper (a convenient and internationally recognized word for motor-caravan), have converted a large van myself and had a truck-sized camper built as the ultimate, so I have formed my opinions about suitability. The main route is tarmac nearly all the way and certainly you do not need four-wheel drive. I do encourage those who wish to build or convert a vehicle themselves, as this gives the activity so much more depth of interest. I really got to know my sons well for the first time when they helped to convert my van. They did all the work and there was much ribald singing and beer drinking.

I am not trying to compete with the numerous conventional guidebooks, nor do I intend to be merely a dull route textbook. I do aim to give you very accurate details of distances, characteristics and facilities on the main and most generally used route and its variations. Also to avoid tedium, I have let myself stray into history, or carpet weaving, autobiography, or landscape. The journey can be enriched by reading up about the various countries before, during and after it and there is a short book list at the end of the book.

I do try to cover all problems that you may encounter and answer your doubts and queries in advance, as well as giving you as many hard-won tips as possible. For instance: who can go; when to go and where to camp; documentation, insurance, finance and costs; the various types of vehicle you can go in; the prime mover; the living quarters; servicing and spares; driving techniques and conditions; stores; cooking equipment; clothing; medical.

Besides all this I will try and convey to you a little about the India and Indians I know and enjoy. I aim above all to get you there safely and wish you a good journey, a journey which will have its trials that eventually lend a sense of adventure and achievement.

2. Who can Go: Manners en Route: Alternatives to the Motor-caravan

Times have changed so much that my answer is, 'Almost anyone can go'. I grew up in the Depression and those who got a job hung on to it rung by rung until they finally retired, often drained of ideas and the ability to enjoy themselves. I find the way young people have the nerve to give up a job and go off in search of adventure a little disturbing, yet I admire it. It is possible for them to take on arduous work to earn very high pay for six months and travel for the other half year.

In an Indian Wild Life Sanctuary I met three young Englishmen who, I considered, had got their lives sorted out in a remarkable manner. They were actually living in two worlds and getting quite a lot of the best out of both. They were studying ornithology, living very simply, and travelling in an ancient Renault van with a modicum of bird-watching equipment – enough, but no more. Two at least were qualified ornithologists and one a botanist. They had done university-sponsored expeditions and were now doing one on their own account. In the other part of the year they had good jobs to which they returned. What a full life! I hope they will marry travelling women and keep it up.

Many young couples take some time off before starting a family, both working and saving for the adventure. Others who have young children take them with them. The children thrive and if they are of school age their parents manage to keep their education going. There is an age limit here as small babies do not stand heat and dust well and have problems with nappies and prickly heat.

We have met emigrants in small and large groups on their way to and from Australia and New Zealand. Students fill in their time before going up to a university. The universities themselves mount expeditions and so do some schools. People go on study grants and on sabbaticals. Many young people drive a little, work a little and earn enough to drive on again. I met a party of intrepid nurses who did this, working and passing on their skills in the more backward hospitals en route.

Those who have most time to do it are those who have retired, but are still young enough to take on an adventure. I have seen travellers in their seventies; it's a matter of pacing oneself. Many pensioners go to revisit countries in which they served, others to lead a fuller, less drab life. How much better this is than to doze away the remaining years before the telly. Some day you'll wake up to find you are dead.

The long-distance motorist gains an absorbing interest. He can read about the countries and he can even build his vehicle so that it becomes an activity in depth and not just a quick dash. So many of us need something more than to hit a little white ball, catch it up and hit it again, or a large coloured one for that matter. I was once playing a polite game of croquet with a very stuffy Frenchman. His ball was black. To liven things up I sent it bounding into the flower beds with my ball, shouting the while, 'Frappez le noir!' When he eventually cooled down he explained that my cry was used to blackball someone aspiring to join a club. Travel can be full of pitfalls.

The British are perhaps the more numerous travellers, but I seem to have met large numbers of Germans, Scandinavians, Dutch and Americans. If you are poor and a good mechanic, you may coax an old deadbeat there and back. If you are rich, you may attract the evil eye and your gleaming monster with all its gadgets may develop gremlins. It's a matter of luck and taking advice.

MANNERS EN ROUTE

I will not dwell on the Hippie. Hippie means different things to different people. I mean derelicts on dope who sponge on people poorer than themselves. How poor the poor are on the route, but they all have pride and a sense of hospitality. Hippies have fouled up the trail a bit and no longer is the white traveller necessarily regarded with respect – it has to be earned. You are a representative of your country, so why not spruce up before crossing a border? The neater you are, the more friendly and accommodating, the more quickly you will cross the eastern borders, which can be tedious. It pays hands down. Man has worn long hair and a beard just as much as he has worn short b. & s., but beards collect the dust and are hot – a judicious trimming is a good thing if you wear one.

Paradoxically in many eastern countries more clothes are worn in spite of the heat, and the greatest modesty is observed. You will not go down with a swing if you wear a bikini – a mini-skirt is also unsuitable for bending over camp chores. You will be considered immodest and fair game, with only yourself to blame, if the village louts get fresh. I don't personally think it's a good idea to dress up as an Indian, Afghan, etc. It always seems to me to be a little patronizing. Be your natural self (see Chapter 12 on Clothing).

You will be shocked at the eastern who uses the countryside unselfconsciously as his W.C. You will shock him far more if you neck in public.

Then there are the hardy annuals – don't offer a Muslim your revolting spam or a sausage. Pork is to him unclean. Have you seen the eastern pig and what he eats in the villages? Don't offer the Hindu beef. He worships the cow in any shape or form, even when she looks like a hatrack. Don't offer the bearded Sikh tobacco in any form, though he'll take a drink any time of day or night – keep firm hold of the bottle. In the west the large dram is measured by the first two fingers. The Sikh or Patiala peg (dram) is measured between the first and last fingers.

When invited to a meal en route or in India, as well you may be, you may sit on the ground supported by a bolster. Try and sit cross-legged if your stiff western bones will permit. It is rude to present the soles of your feet. You will learn to eat with your hands and will eventually never want to use implements again for such food, but it must be the right hand. The left is confined to purposes of hygiene.

It is vitally important to keep calm and at the same time warm and friendly. The easterner with his hospitality is also very warm in his friendliness (see Chapter 23). But he is more emotional, so that if you show impatience and are cross, his smiles will evaporate and he will swing to the opposite extreme. His reactions are complex as well as emotional. He will be sorrowfully cast down at your displeasure and this will make him furious.

English is spoken by many people on your way and in a crisis someone who knows a little always seems to turn up. In India it is the second language of the educated man. It is important though to learn a few words of greeting in the countries you visit. To do so is more significant than you may realize. It means bridging the gap and going at least half-way to meet the people you have come to see. Your mispronounced words will be met with smiles, not of derision but of real pleasure –

warm smiles. Then nothing is too much trouble and you will find even shopping great fun (see Appendix II). The Muslim and Hindu religions both teach hospitality in a way beyond that of the cold, jealous West.

Phrase books are still a bit antiquated, though our Turkish one was obviously written by a dipsomaniac. We can ask for red or white wine, but never a drink of water or milk.

One point I would emphasize is that unless you are a confirmed loner, or travelling in a group, you should get yourself a 'travelling man or woman', or better still a wife or husband who loves travelling as much as you do. Above all, do not saddle yourself with a nag. Generally speaking the more pokey your wagon, the greater the strain on perfect love.

ALTERNATIVES TO THE MOTOR CARAVAN

Towed Caravans. These are really unsuitable for this form of travel as one meets rough roads in places, high winds and blizzards far more severe than in England. If it is the only way you can go, then you need something like a Land-Rover to tow it and a very good van. I have known the ordinary light type used in England break up en route.

A Car with a Tent. This method is perfectly feasible, but not very comfortable. A tent is no good in cold or heat and can be easily overrun in areas where security is suspect. In any case, it lacks privacy if you are staying long in an area. If you have to travel this way you would probably be wisest to stop in hotels and motels en route, the greater expense being offset by the fact that you will probably make the journey faster than in a camper. There is accommodation to be found in most towns along the route.

By Coach or Bus. Apart from the regular bus services that run from Munich to Teheran, there are numerous companies that run tours as far as Kathmandu in Nepal. I have met many of their vehicles on the way and they always seem to be most efficiently run by competent drivers and tour leaders. It is a wonderful way of travelling with a group of like-minded people and the tours are geared to different financial levels, from those that travel with a group of tents to those that stay in hotels at varying prices. The cost is probably about the same as if you go independently, but you do not have the capital cost of a vehicle to find. For further information, I suggest you get in touch with Trailfinders Ltd., 46–8 Earl's Court Road, London W8 (01 937 9631), who specialize in this sort of travel.

3. *When to Travel and Where to Camp*

The Best Time To Go, India in the Winter, India in the Summer, Kashmir and Nepal, Monsoons, Time Needed for the Journey, Night Halts in Europe, Camps in Asia, Camping Wild, Tents, A Day's Run.

The Best Time To Go. I would advocate a round trip of six months, leaving in mid-October and returning in April. This means that you avoid excessive heat in southern Europe and from Afghanistan onwards. In the heights of Turkey nights will be cold, but not impossibly so. You stand a good chance of not meeting even freak snowy weather and at the same time the heavy rains of early October in Turkey and Iran should be over.

To return earlier than April is foolish. It can be done, but much of Turkey and Iran will be under deep snow from late December till mid-March. The roads are cleared by snow ploughs, but they are dangerous. You want to avoid snow, if you possibly can as you are not a toboggan. I have twice returned in early February, but only got through by good luck. You may have no choice, but if you have, opt for a later date.

If you plan to spend the summer in India, then travel in the same seasons as for winter, but in reverse as it were, i.e. out in April and home in October.

India in the Winter. Pakistan and northern India will be enjoying delightfully clear, sunny weather for ninety-five per cent of the time. On average, November will be like a very warm summer's day at home. December, January and early February will be pleasantly warm by day, but cool by night except for Peshawar, Rawalpindi and Quetta in Pakistan where it will be very cold – see Chapter 20. Frost is rare, but an inadequately insulated camper will be uncomfortably cold – see Chapters 5 and 7 on the need for insulation. I suggest, if your camper is not well insulated, that you head for south India until the spring. The farther south, the narrower is the land with the sea's temperate influence closing in. It will be really warm down south – only a little cooler than in the summer, though nights will be pleasant. It is more humid and relaxing than in the north – never stinking hot at any time of year, but a bit unpleasant in the hot weather.

India in the Summer. Parts of India and Pakistan are almost intolerably hot during the summer and it is in general the worst time of year to travel. But these countries are more beautiful then and foliage and flowers gayer, while exotic fruit is at its best. However well you insulate your camper, it will be hotter than living in a house built against the heat. If you are a wealthy nabob you may have air conditioning on your vehicle, but this opens up all sorts of problems of charging batteries. If you are elderly and retired or have children with you, go for the winter. I think this is good advice to the young too, though they will survive the heat more easily: but why make a holiday a survival test?

If you find it too warm in the south, take a breather in the lovely Nilgiri Hills there. They are very pleasant in the summer, though cold at night in the winter. You will have to dodge the monsoon which strikes at different times on different hill slopes. The monsoons are not cold, but wet and depressing.

Kashmir and Nepal. If your aim is to spend your time in Kashmir or the uplands of Nepal, then by all means go for the summer. Kathmandu can be very hot then, though there are excellent trek arrangements for living in the cool uplands. I am told you really can poach an egg on the pavement there, but for God's sake don't eat it. It is a dirty, fly-blown area and there are the high tide marks of foundered hippies and their vehicles. It's actually silly to go to Kashmir for the winter unless you go for the skiing which is good. From early May until the end of September the weather is lovely, but after that there is a lot of rain and snow and the famous Valley can look extraordinarily depressing.

Monsoons. The rainy season strikes the south early in June and moves slowly northwards, though the incidence is uncertain nowadays in an era of climatic change. Dodge the rains if you can. When it rains, roads and bridges are frequently washed away.

Time Needed for the Journey. The best run I have done on my pre-ferred route was a return trip from Peshawar to England in fifteen and a half days, cruising at about 53 m.p.h. This is nothing remarkable. I think three weeks is a sensible estimate from England to Delhi, if you don't stop much on the way. If you do, you may run out of the optimum weather. For more detailed information see Chapters 14 to 21.

Motor rallies can do it in seven days, but experts check and retune the engines at night and cars are looked after assiduously. The driver and his co-driver go at more than twice the overall speed of most campers, so on this run, on average, they will strike less bad weather. Competitors in the London to Sydney Rally some years ago described it as a piece of cake. It can be. We met the scouting team for the next rally the following year and went over a suggested forest route we knew well, winding from sacred Hardwar on the Ganges to Kotwara and eventually to the main road from Lucknow to Delhi. Knowing that forest track rallies are popular in Europe, I hoped that this would provide a little more bread and butter and sometimes just bread, rather than all that cake. We met the team later in Delhi. Their car looked very battered and they looked thoughtful.

Night Halts in Europe. Halts on the way through Europe are easiest in the numerous service stations on the motorways. There are usually no restrictions or charge and most of the Raststätte have long bays for juggernauts into which one can tuck oneself. In Yugoslavia they do find their service stations good areas for storing their surplus litter and for pouring out old engine oil, but in the main they are very fine.

Greek motor-camps are generally delightful and set in gardens, so we opt for one, though camping wild is allowed.

Camps in Asia (see Appendix IV). In Turkey there are many motor camps round Istamboul, as far as Ankara and all round the Aegean and Mediterranean coasts. They are good and clean and have plenty of hot water. Some are owned by petrol companies and some are private. East of Ankara there are one or two stopping places, but no real camps except on the Black Sea coast. Petrol stations anywhere provide a rather noisy haven. In Turkey they are regarded as 'neutral' territory. One is always warned against camping wild in this country, but it can be done – see p. 14.

14 When to Travel and Where to Camp

In Iran it is usually safe to camp wild. There are one or two camps indicated in tourist pamphlets, but they are poor. The petrol stations are usually rather small. Beware of the Inns as they are called. They are clean and well run and provide good meals, but they may make you take a room, even if you only want to sleep in the car park.

In Afghanistan you are welcome to park in hotel grounds the whole way through. The authorities encourage it and the fee is small. Public order is not as good as it used to be and violence and robbery are not uncommon. In other words take the parking accommodation offered by the government: they know the risks.

Many hotels will let you do the same in Pakistan and India and there are always Dak Bungalows (rest houses), Engineers' Bungalows, Circuit Bungalows, etc. In actual practice these cannot be booked in advance. It just doesn't work. Most of them will allow you to park in the grounds and use what simple facilities there are. The politer you are, the better you will be received.

It is usually possible to camp in controlled areas in wild life parks and camping wild in southern India is not difficult, as there are forested areas where you can conceal yourself. Northern India is flatter and more open so that it is generally impossible to camp wild unnoticed. You will be mobbed by friendly, inquisitive crowds in greater numbers than you would believe possible. This applies too to petrol stations, but the owner will usually clear crowds away for you. There is an official camp in Delhi.

Camping Wild. 'Can one camp in the wild by night?' is a familiar question. Yes, oh yes, is my answer. That is what it's all about. I have, however, worked out a few rough and ready rules, based partly on military experience and partly on having travelled and walked over miles of the fascinating, shaley uplands.

Let us put things into perspective. A journey to India is little more dangerous than shopping in a crowded English town. In eastern Anatolia there might just be a few Kurds to make you curdle or a few nomads in Afghanistan. Therefore, start looking for your wild camp near sunset. The road may be raised above the plain so a pull-off may be a little hard to find. Choose one early rather than late, as after dark it is hard to see sideways, i.e. choose the first reasonable place. Walk it, ostensibly to spend a penny or something, noting whether the ground is as hard as it looks. It often isn't and rain may turn it into a bog. If the surface feels hard, is well sown with large pebbles or a binding of desert weed, then it will be O.K. even in the rare event of rainfall.

Never camp in a watercourse, anywhere, ever. The drier the watercourse, the more prone it is to spate in a soil-eroded country. In such semi-desert areas the water runs wild from neighbouring mountains, although you may have had no rain on the plain. I know so many instances of cars being washed away on an Irish bridge or from a 'dry' river bed. An Irish bridge is a slight dip in the road, made of concrete if you are lucky. This is designed to let a stream or river pass over the road, but in bad weather the water can be so deep that you can't see the road in spite of marker posts.

Never park on hard-looking clay sub-soil, generally of a red colour. It will turn to absolute glue in a shower. All I am really telling you is to exercise common sense, but sometimes one hasn't much of that left when one is tired.

Having chosen your haven get back into the camper and drink high octane 'char' with your companions and look about you. (It is a good thing to carry plenty of tea in thermoses as a quick restorer while driving.) You have told no one you are stopping for the night. Everyone will assume you are going on to some sleazy tourist hotel. It is very cold in the uplands and people will soon seek shelter. One or two shepherds may be filtering away to some mud-walled enclosure, ghostly in their squared-off, white, beaten felt coats. When all has settled down and it is darkening, pull off without lights and park reasonably level. Don't pull off far, but just out of the line of headlights, using the lie of the road to assist you if possible in your choice of place. Make yourselves lightproof and cook the evening meal. Go to bed by seven p.m. having set the alarm for four or five a.m. – early bed is no hardship, for it is dark by five p.m. in these latitudes.

You will not regret this upland camp. Slipping out of the camper you look up at incredibly bright diamonds, billions of them sharpened by the rare air. You want to spread your hands up to grasp them so far away, but seeming so close. If there be a moon, it is almost bright enough to read by. The desert is so quiet that it hums to itself and the stars sing below the pitch of sound. You hear the distant howl of a wolf, thin, clear and high. The far-off village dogs yearn for the moon in high, piping yowls, and the desert is sweet with aromatic herbs.

The biggest safety factor is that no one knows you are there. Should you camp two nights in the same place, you might attract trouble. Bivouac tents are easily overrun, so large campers are safer. No one knows how many people may be inside. In the Autumn of 1976 a bus-load on their way to India broke down in eastern Turkey and had to stay two nights in one spot. On the second they were surrounded by Kurds armed with automatics and stripped of all they had.

Above all don't leave your possessions scattered about. In the uplands even a red jerrican is riches to be envied, so lock up carefully at night. Should you ever tangle with raiders, be firm and angry. Sneak thieves are gutless and can sometimes be confounded. In Afghanistan, don't camp near the low black tents of the nomads who are often armed and answer to no man. Murder is endemic.

Tents. These remarks above do not mean that it is impossible to use tents based on a vehicle (see p. 9), but you would be wise as far as possible to camp in a protected area such as a hotel's grounds, a petrol station, etc. Petrol stations out in the country in Turkey usually have gravel surfaces into which pegs can be driven. In Herat, Afghanistan, (see Chapter 19) use the Park Hotel rather than the Herat Hotel as the latter is surrounded by tarmac. The Park Hotel is first on your left as you turn into the Russian concrete road for Kandahar. Wherever you are keep all loose possessions locked up in your vehicle, and remember that tents are particularly vulnerable to flood water.

A Day's Run. On the wilder parts of the journey with long runs between halting places an early start is essential, especially as in winter the day-light hours are short – it is usually dark by 5 p.m. local time. To achieve this without friction you need an alarm clock and a rigid routine in which everyone, whether you are a pair or a party, has an exact role. This way you can get off in good time without forgetting important things like checking the vehicle or doing the washing up. How lovely are the early morning drives. A pale fox crosses the road as the animal world surrenders its kingdom to cruel man. No sign of your passage remains, but you have stolen a bit of desert and sky all for yourselves.

Those who have the misfortune to be in uninsulated tin boxes tend to drive long into the night, warming themselves with the engine heater and then when the sun warms the roof, park and go to sleep. This can be dangerous as you are open to molestation and certainly harassment out of curiosity, acquisitiveness or impishness. The desert always sprouts small boys in the daytime like mischievous goblins from nowhere and as you drop off to sleep there will be a loud bang on your paintwork and a chuckle. In any case driving by night is a damn silly way of seeing a country, more fatiguing and hazardous. I drive every bit of the daylight when I'm on the big run and sometimes make a kind of lone rally of it. In the last two years I have twice done fourteen hours non-stop at the wheel save for halts for a pee or petrol. One can only drive such long hours if you have special shock absorbing seats e.g. The Bostrom type (see Chapter 6).

In principle it's better to stop at sunset. It would be a long chance if you stopped in the middle of an ambush. Whereas if you motor late at night you might pick one up. Such misadventures are rare, but one is enough, so raise the odds by using common sense.

If you leave your camper unattended, lock everything including external gear if you must have it. I try and appoint someone to mount guard while I'm away – there is always a stander-by who will be glad to earn a small coin. Your spare wheel generally is external. Give great thought to its positioning for accessibility and then chain and padlock it. It will then take a thief a little longer to steal it. One traveller who was wont to blacken his lungs with tobacco nipped round the corner for a packet of cigarettes. On returning he realized his car was much lower. He'd lost four wheels in five minutes flat. But this was in Italy where fingers can be as light as operas are airy.

4. *Documentation, Finance and Costs*

PERSONAL DOCUMENTS – Passports, Visas, Pakistan–India Border Pass, Inoculation Certificates. DOCUMENTS FOR THE VEHICLE – Motoring Organizations, Driving Licences, Carnets, Customs, Insurance. FINANCE AND COSTS – Form T., Bank of England, Travellers' Cheques, Rates of Exchange, Banks, Banking Hours, Budgeting.

I would suggest you consult this chapter whenever you come to a difficult border. After Austria, border crossings become a sort of red tape game – fun for the officials one assumes, but most galling for the tourist. Unnecessary numbers of people are involved as a part of the 'jobs for the boys' effort.

PERSONAL DOCUMENTS

Passports. To begin with you will need a large number of passport photos for each person. If you intend to travel often, I would suggest at least three dozen.

The farther east you go, the larger and more numerous the stamps on your passport. If you are the driver, a trip to India and back will use up more than half a normal sized one. So get the extra large or B size for which you pay correspondingly more. It is worth it since an existing passport cannot be enlarged – one has to get a new one each time.

Incidentally, be careful to get your own passport back at a border, not someone else's. I've known it happen.

Visas. Visas are required for Afghanistan. Write to the Afghan Embassy (address in F.O. booklet issued with your passport) for application forms, usually three per person, enclosing a stamped self-addressed envelope (S.A.E.). If you don't enclose it, they won't reply. A passport photo is needed for each form which should be sent in with your passport and valid inoculation certificates for smallpox, cholera and typhoid, together with a postal order for the fee and a S.A.E. At the time of writing this fee is £2 a head. Visas can be Tourist or Transit and can be taken up any time during the ensuing three months. It takes about a week to get the visas by post and two visits if you go personally. On your return journey the visas can be got either in Peshawar or Quetta at the Afghan Visa Office. One cannot get a return visa from London, but the office in Peshawar is quick and helpful and the formalities are generally completed in a morning. Avoid the Consular Section of the Embassy in Islamabad. They will never do it under three days and the officials are rude and slightly mad.

If you go via Bulgaria, you will need a visa. It is better to get this from the Bulgarian Embassy in London at a cost of 75p. rather than on the border for £5. You do not need photos or health certificates. The Embassy states that if you plan to stay a week or two in the country on your way, you do not need a visa, but many such travellers have had to buy visas at the border before being allowed to enter the country.

Pakistan–India Border Pass. At the moment of writing visas are not required for holders of British Passports entering India. However, travellers crossing from Pakistan to India and vice versa need a special road pass from the Pakistan authorities. On the outward journey this pass can be got from the Embassy in London – it takes eight weeks. Alternatively it can be obtained from the Lahore branch of the Ministry of Kashmir and Home Affairs, during your journey. If you have a military rank that is shown on your passport, it is better to go direct to the Secretariat in Islamabad. The Ministry is in the first lot of government buildings on the right-hand side of Secretariat Road. On the return journey the permit can be obtained from the passport authorities after crossing back into Pakistan.

Inoculation Certificates. As indicated, you cannot get the Afghan visas without up-to-date inoculation certificates for smallpox, cholera and typhoid. It is in any case important to be protected and you will have to produce them and have them stamped on entering Afghanistan on the outward journey and Iran on the homeward one. Otherwise your journey will come to a full stop. Until recently, coming from India to Iran valid cholera certificates were not considered enough. This was due to Indians getting the certificate and not the needle, which led to unfortunate outbreaks of cholera in Iran. One's passport was confiscated until one had swallowed a few large capsules and one had to go on one's journey with the driver full of unspecified drugs. This practice had stopped, so far as certificates backed by a reputable doctor were concerned, on our last journey home. If your return is more than six months after your initial cholera inoculation, you must have a booster and your certificate stamped. This can be done at the High Commission Hospital in Delhi – the one service they are allowed to render travellers – and their stamp is acceptable.

Besides the compulsory inoculations I would suggest that you are guarded against polio and tetanus. Anti-'flu inoculation is worth considering, since 'flu is common in India in a mild form. It does seem to be some protection against the common cold which is always a threat, particularly if you are a large party or travelling with children.

DOCUMENTS FOR THE VEHICLE

Motoring Organizations. Although you do not need the help of the motoring organizations for booking your vehicle across the Channel you do need it for securing the documents mentioned below, so one member of the party should join. Remember, however, that the various schemes of cover they offer only apply to your journey in Europe, i.e. a third of your trip, and are only valid for the calendar year in which they are taken out.

Driving Licences. Anyone who may drive needs an International Driving Licence, and a special one for Pakistan. These you can get through a motoring organization which will require the number of your current licence and two photos.

Carnets. The International Carnet de Passage is required for entry into Pakistan and India. This is valid for a year from the date of issue and you can keep your vehicle for a period of up to six months in these countries. The carnet should be obtained through your motoring organization and you will need to furnish a banker's guarantee of indemnity to refund any expenses the organization may incur should you fail to re-export your vehicle within the allotted time. The guarantee is usually

250 per cent of the estimated value of the vehicle. In India a very heavy duty is levied on any vehicle which does not leave the country. It may be seized by the Customs should one attempt to take it out after the proper date. To dispose of it there, you must sell it to the State Trading Corporation at a poor price. The fact that it is then sold at a high one is your bad luck. In exceptional circumstances such as scientific or cultural research the carnet can be extended for a further six months. It is not easy and entails many weary visits to obscure and dusty offices. Do not think you can sell your car for a bomb anywhere along the line, even in Nepal. Those days are over. You can however leave your vehicle with the Customs at a seaport if you want to extend your journey eastwards or elsewhere and return to take it out of the country.

Customs. Details of your car will be entered in your passport at the Greek and Turkish borders.

On entering Iran you have to buy an entry permit for 120 rials (about £1) and sign a guarantee undertaking to take the vehicle out within six months. You can use a carnet, but one valid for Iran needs a banker's guarantee for about 300 per cent. If you can afford it, do so. It is much quicker and involves less formalities and form filling by the officials who get very disagreeable at the prospect of much writing and tend to treat you as a poor white. You sign a customs declaration for your other possessions – the chief interest is arms or drugs – and a very thorough search will be made of your vehicle on the return journey, coming in from Afghanistan.

Entering Afghanistan you are given three copies of a form to fill in and no carbon! You declare details of your camper, cameras, transistors, etc. One copy must be shown and filled in all over again as you leave the country. You have to declare your foreign currency and show receipts for travellers' cheques cashed, when you leave. A very thorough search is made of vehicles and bus passengers' baggage on the border with Iran on the return journey, ostensibly to prevent drug smuggling (a government monopoly) and the export of arms and antiques. Each traveller has to pay 100 Afghanis (75p.) at the passport office for leave to exit from the country, in any direction.

When filling in forms on these borders carry your carnet with you for quick reference for vehicle details and your log book. Don't forget a biro for writing all this bumph and your spectacles if you need them.

Insurance. You need a Green Card from your insurance company to cover your journey through Europe. Get one for your return journey too. It is very expensive to do local insurance at borders.

Turkish insurance for Asiatic Turkey can be got in Istamboul – the word is Sigorta and there are offices on the left of the main highway before you enter the city. Insurance is important as foreigners come off very badly *vis-à-vis* the law in an accident.

Insurance is compulsory on the borders of Iran and Afghanistan. You will not be allowed in without it. There are offices close to the Customs and it is quick and inexpensive. In Iran Third Party is sufficient. In Afghanistan you have to insure your passengers as well.

Pakistan insurance can be taken out in Peshawar and in Amritsar for India. Insurance is nationalized in the latter country, but the international companies act as agents for the government. Amritsar is such a maelstrom that I prefer to by-pass it and go to the Royal Assurance unit in Barakumba Road, just off Connaught Circus in New Delhi. Third Party is again cheap, but one is out on a limb from the border to Delhi.

I have tried to insure for the whole journey in England, but no one is ever very clued up and any quotations have been wildly expensive.

FINANCE AND COSTS

Form T. – Bank of England. The amount of money you have to spend depends on you and your bank. Grindlays Bank looks after me like a mother and their foreign department arranges for the necessary application to the Bank of England for permission to cash cheques through their agents abroad over and above the normal travel allowance which is no longer sufficient for a long journey for two people. If you are a large party you may not need this as six or seven use no more fuel than two. Should you need permission to draw extra funds, be modest in your requests. If you are greedy you may spoil it for others.

Travellers' Cheques. I would advise taking most of your foreign allowance in this form, for safety reasons apart from the fact that you are only allowed a strictly limited amount of sterling cash with you. I usually buy dollar cheques in case of a further devaluation in sterling. Travellers' Cheques can be cashed on the cross-Channel ferries and used to pay the fares on your return journey. You get a better rate for European currencies than at banks and border exchanges on these ferries.

Rates of Exchange. I would advise you to get the ruling rates of exchange for the various countries you will pass through before you leave. The rates will vary, probably downwards, but it does give you a rough guide for making your calculations before getting to a border, thus saving time and confusion. It is a good tip to change enough money on the outward journey to cover probable expenses on the return one. Then if there is a decline in the value of the pound or the dollar, you can get home. Hide all your spare cash in small sums in different places in your vehicle where thieves cannot easily find them. Don't carry all your money on you.

Banks. There are exchange banks on all borders up to and including the Turkish/Iranian frontier. Remember that on the Turkish side the banks do not open early. It is wise to be patient and wait for them as once you are in Turkey it is very difficult to change Travellers' Cheques – they are only handled by certain mercantile banks such as the Ottoman and the Iş Bankasi in a few large towns. You can change a small amount at the camps near Istamboul and some hotels will deal in foreign currency, not cheques. The Turkish unit of currency is the lira (pl. lirasi) divided into a hundred kurus.

As well as at the borders you can change Travellers' Cheques at Bank Melli branches all over Iran. In Teheran I would use the money changers, a kind of grey market down the Avenue Firdausi. The Bank Melli takes a year and a day. The unit of currency is the rial.

The border between Iran and Afghanistan is a problem as they are always changing the rules. There is no bank for outgoing travellers on the Iranian side and there are no dealings there in Afghan currency. The Bank Melli functions for returning travellers. The bank is beside the Customs counter.

On the Afghan side of the border there is sometimes a bank working and sometimes not. Customs officials will change Iranian rials for you at a poor rate and car insurance can be done in foreign currency (cash). For this reason we bring extra rials with us from the Turkish–Iranian border. If one has any left over after the return journey they can be changed at the border on the way out to Turkey. If you are not in a hurry or need more Afghanis (the Afghan unit of currency), go to the Afghan Bank in Herat for a better exchange rate, though the procedure is long and cumbersome. Remember you will need Afs. 50 (40p.) for tolls before that city.

Don't count on finding a black market money changer and their rates are not as good as the bank's. *Do not go into any Afghan bazaar* to change money except in Kabul and then by day only. To show money in the by-ways is highly dangerous. Money changers in Kabul will give you good rates against sterling or dollars for Pakistani and Indian rupees, but remember you are not supposed to import these into either country, where the exchange is fixed artificially.

There are banks on both sides of the Afghan–Pakistan border and an insurance office for your return journey through Afghanistan. It is not, and I repeat not, worth changing money with the black market dealers on the Pakistan side. Their rates are not good. I think it is only their persistence that enables them to do business at all.

There is no bank on the Pakistan side of the Indo–Pakistan border. Any business must be done in Lahore.

There is a branch of the State Bank of India on the Indian side of the border. You will have to declare your currency as you enter India and obtain a certificate from the money changer for each transaction you make. On production of these certificates when you return home you can change your surplus rupees, if any, into foreign exchange with the exception of Pakistani rupees. There are black market money changers near the barrier who will give you these rupees, but the rates are poor and the notes suspect.

In India you can change money at the State Bank and other reputable establishments as well as hotels, but it is sometimes difficult in the provinces. It is better to do your transactions in Delhi. Black market rates are very little better than the official ones. Their chief attraction is that the transaction is quick. Indian banks are slower than the Mills of God.

Bills for accommodation in five-star hotels must be paid by foreigners in foreign currency or travellers' cheques. This applies also to house-boats in Kashmir. Wild Life Parks have, paradoxically, no facilities for changing foreign currency and will not accept travellers' cheques.

Banking Hours. In Turkey these are much the same as in Europe. In Iran the same applies except that the banks are shut on Fridays and open on Sundays. In Afghanistan the hours are short as banks close at noon. They too are shut on Fridays. Pakistan and India are like Europe except that Pakistan banks are only open for a short time on Friday mornings.

Budgeting. In a book like this it is fatal to make you out a daily budget for food and fuel. Some people eat twice as much as others. Some take only a few stores with them and others almost enough for the duration, depending on storage room and inclination. I am not going to discuss food in Europe where it is much more expensive than in England because you can get round this by taking cooked fresh food and a tin or two, from home. Once you leave Europe, you will find that prices for food average out much the same as in this country. I have found this to be so over a period of twelve years' long distance motoring up to date. From Turkey onwards fruit, vegetables, meat etc. are not expensive, except for Teheran where oil-boom prices rule. Don't fall into the trap of thinking that India is a very cheap country. Basic products have not gone up in the last two years, but fresh food costs about the same as in England and is of poor to very poor quality. Tinned goods are expensive. Really drinkable liquor is prohibitive. Good class hotels cost as much as London. The few camp sites are cheap.

I therefore suggest that you allow a daily rate the same as each member would expect to spend on food in England, plus twenty-five per cent for emergency.

Again, for similar reasons, I'm not going to make you out tables for fuel consumption in various vehicles. It is absolutely essential that you try your vehicle out thoroughly in England before you take on the journey, with all your baggage loaded as part of the trial. Your type of driving may be quite different from the next man's and your fuel consumption figures may differ from his by as much as forty per cent. Again a square box body or high roof loading will create wind resistance and you will return a poorer figure. Half the journey is in high altitudes which will influence your consumption figures slightly for the worse. From the Sea of Marmora to the Khyber I would expect an average of ten per cent increased consumption on account of the high average altitude. If you do as I suggest you will arrive at a far more accurate figure than any inflexible table can give you: work out how many gallons you will need overall to cover your estimated mileage at your own rate of consumption with allowance for altitude. Then allow twenty-five per cent more for running about in towns, etc.

Find out the price of petrol/diesel and lubricants on the way and at your destination. Your motoring organization will be able to give you an idea. While writing this I got the answer within twenty-four hours. Expect a slightly higher price during your journey because prices are always rising. The only countries where they have altered little in recent years are Iran and Afghanistan where they are about a third of English prices. In Turkey and India the price will vary with your distance from the main centres. In the other countries, prices are uniform. Outside Europe diesel costs roughly half as much as petrol. With your personal estimated consumption figures and the motoring organization's price list, you can work out how much money you will need for fuel in each country. Keep a record of prices on the way out, to calculate your costs for the return journey, again allowing a margin.

You must remember to allow for car ferry passages for yourselves and your vehicle – the cost of the latter depends on its length. I cannot give you a reliable figure. It has increased so much of late. Get this figure from your motoring association just before leaving.

The current charge for a Green Insurance Card is £4 per month or less, for Third Party. Allow £50 at least for insurance and road tolls en route.

You have to have a certain amount of money (approx. £150 per person) with you to enter Afghanistan – the exact amount will be indicated on your visa form. Presumably you would in any case have this much on you either on your way to India or on your way home. The Afghans merely want to be sure you won't founder in their country.

Medicines and amusements will cost you much the same as in England, except that cinemas in India are much cheaper. How much money you need is a personal matter.

For repairs and servicing en route I usually allow £200 for the round trip, hoping not to use it all. Labour charges out of Europe are substantially lower than in England; spare parts will probably cost more. I suggest that you arrange with your bank for it to forward extra funds should you have a serious breakdown and allow for this when making your Form T application. I have done this twice, once to Germany and once to Iran.

At the risk of pointing out the obvious, may I suggest you look into the possibilities of letting your house or flat while you are away, via an agent. The income from this might go quite a long way towards financing your trip.

Precis of Costs

Daily Food	..	Rate per head as in England plus 25%.
Fuel	..	Based on latest prices from motoring organization and estimated overall consumption, plus 25%.
Sea Transit	..	Up-to-the-moment figures – see above.
Insurance	..	Green card for outward and homeward journey.
		£60 from Asiatic Turkey out and back together with tolls.
Medicines etc.	..	As in England (when not under the National Health).
Repairs	..	£200 with you and facility to get more if necessary.

5. Stock Campers versus Building your Own

Coach-built on a Chassis, Van Conversions, Raising Roof. MAKES OF CAMPER, BUILDING YOUR OWN.

Roughly, stock built campers fall into three categories – like Caesar's Gaul.

Coach-built on a Chassis. Obviously these are the most expensive. They can be huge and if so, you need a jumbo purse. They will have standing head-room for all except giraffes, and numerous gadgets. Their great advantage is that you can get a light bus chassis with a speedy back axle ratio and good soft suspension.

Van Conversions. These, if big enough to stand up in, are probably the most economic buy. If not too big they can be your general purpose vehicle too.

Raising Roof. The smaller vehicles generally have various types of raising roof. They can be cold to live in and flimsy in the roof section, apart from the fact that they may take some time to set up at the end of a tiring day. The pivoting type of roof is no good in a high wind and one may have to call all hands on deck and close down in the middle of the night if a wind gets up – I know, I've done it. However, the small vehicles are probably the answer for the young or the serpentine or those with a small purse.

MAKES OF CAMPER

Land-Rover British Leyland: The most popular English camper in several forms is based on the long wheelbase (LWB) Land-Rover, petrol or diesel – the $2\frac{1}{4}$ litre diesel can return 32 m.p.g. Unless you plan a special archaeological cross-country expedition, you do not need four-wheel drive (FWD), so it becomes an expensive luxury on a normal India run. FWD only pulls out of mud or snow if the tyres grip and cross-country tyres are not good long distance road runners. The Land-Rover is best working from a base camp where there is ever-ready service. It is a small vehicle so travellers, be they a family, a group, or a couple tend to pile everything on the roof which is most dangerous. If a group use it as a parent from which they camp in bivouac tents, then again this rugged donkey is rendered almost unroadworthy with weird and wonderful roof structures and trailers.

Ford and Bedford Conversions. These are more comfortable in the larger sizes and have more room to live in and keep your stores. They do very well on this journey and are used by the overland companies, who also use converted army trucks.

Commer. I am chary of recommending Commer vehicles because I suspect that service facilities are not good in the countries that you will travel through.

Volkswagen. The most popular of all is the German Volkswagen series of campers based on the microbus, particularly the Westphalia and the Combi. They are no more perfect than the English, being extremely poky with raising roofs. When master shaves, the little woman stays out in the rain. On long trips close and constant proximity might turn them into Divorce Wagons. They are handy and fast, though slightly unstable. Their fuel consumption is not light. Being air-cooled one does not have to bother about frost, but this is not all advantage. Where temperatures are constantly changing, at one moment the engine runs too cold and the next too hot. They lack water-cooling's inherent stability, but they seem to get by.

Mercedes. There is a case for Mercedes vehicles. They are more expensive, but there is a number of very fine diesel models.

Americans. Few can afford such vehicles like the Winnebago Chieftain initially and still fewer can bear the cost of fuel. They are also impractical for the eastern run because they are bred for great, smooth American highways with flat mocamps – camper rallies, all poker and bourbon.

I have inspected one in Indian conditions. It was bought second-hand – still at a large price – and was owned by a charming English couple, an ex-army officer and his wife, a nurse. They were taking it out to Australia to live in until they got a job. The vehicle's great rear-overhang kept it off the side roads and jungle roads. It was crammed with bulky electrical appliances. These could be run on the batteries for one night only after a journey and then it was plug-in. There was no manual alternative. This is no good for camping wild, or for more primitive camps for more than one night's stay. The whole vehicle was too compartmented – nowhere could all your friends sit down round a sizeable table and drink jungle juice in the jungle. Its space thus wastefully disposed had surprisingly small lockerage.

Transferring from my vehicle, I found it very hot, lacking insulation. The wife was almost in tears. In two days the Indian dust of decay had got into the tweed covers and shaggy carpet. She could not get rid of the smell of decayed pi-dogs and vultures.

They were cruising at 80 m.p.h. in Iran, but when they got to an expensive fuel area, dropped down to 35 m.p.h. Do not be gulled by quoted figures for consumption in some magazines. You can't pour it much faster direct on to the ground.

Japanese. These have only recently come on the market and I have not seen them 'in action'. At first sight they look a little flimsy, but are probably economic to run.

BUILDING YOUR OWN

I have been as poor as a church mouse most of my life, with many drains on pin-money pay, so I look to saving the beginner's pocket. It is true though, that I have more recently improved my lot to be no poorer than a church rat and lately perhaps a church bat. Why spend vast sums on gadgety week-end campers like goldfish bowls? The young of today take to D.I.Y. like ducks to water. Why not buy a stout van and build the furnishings yourself? It will be a tough, workaday vehicle which will, if looked after, take you nearly round the clock. In building it you will have started long distance motoring from the bottom end and this is the way to get full enjoyment out of it.

Better still, get a chassis and build the shell as well. Then you can have an individual vehicle like no one else's. When you get to the rat stage, buy a truck or light bus chassis and start bigger. If you get to the bat stage, you really can take off.

All campers are a compromise, but if you build for yourself you can make something nearer your ideal. Even these may attract V.A.T. nowadays, so you should consult your local customs and excise officer.

My suggestions below in Chapters 6, 7 and 8, apply both to D.I.Y. and stock campers. Where you have to take the ready-made you can often adapt and improve. The following pages are really meant as a kind of yardstick.

6. *The Prime Mover*

Size, Diesel v. Petrol, Air Cleaner, Fuel Filter, Back Axle and Gearbox, Compression, Suspension, Clearance, Fuel Tank, Tyres, Seats, Mirrors and Horns, Lights, Flashers and Washers, Fire Extinguisher, Towing Rings.

Size. Big vehicles are surprisingly easy to handle and ideal for a long journey. Double back wheels and a forward control cab take you into a new sphere. If you go big, you pay more and you have to cope with a greater thirst – this at a time when the Arabs, for so long content to sit on sand and look at goats and camels, are now sitting on oil too. You need room if you are going to live in a vehicle for a long time or want to take a lot of stores with you, whether you are a couple or a group. On the other hand a big camper may not fit between decks if you are travelling on a ship that is not a motor ferry and its freight charges will be higher than for a smaller vehicle. I refer to journeys on to Australia and New Zealand from India or to Africa or South America.

Diesel v. Petrol. Diesel fuel has not gone up as much in price as petrol in foreign countries and as the consumption is more economic the balance tends to favour the diesel, whose engine is inherently tough and long lasting. If you go diesel, go as large as you can. With smaller diesels you have to put up with a howl like a banshee, even if you insulate as much as possible. This noise does increase fatigue – you notice it when you stop for border formalities.

Diesels are more expensive initially, so that you may have to motor for some time before you close the gap in cost. More important is the fact that they have poor acceleration, especially at low speed. I would advise you, having bought a diesel, to drive it on an English motorway at an uncrowded time to get to know it. Then you will be less likely to do a dangerous overtake on some vast mountain road where you will find big, overloaded and underserviced vehicles belching black smoke and moving at a snail's pace. I hate edging past some monster, driving ear to ear with a once-distant bend coming nearer and nearer. After all, great acceleration is the finest safety device a car can have barring that of good brakes. The petrol vehicle is easier to drive due to its greater acceleration and is quieter.

Air Cleaner. An oil bath air cleaner is essential. You are motoring in dusty countries and other types of air cleaner admit a great deal of dust to clog up the works. You should change the oil in the air cleaner at least twice as often as you do in Europe and even more frequently if you are on unmade forest tracks.

Fuel Filter. A large diesel type fuel filter in addition to the standard one can be fitted on to a petrol engine to protect it against bad fuel. This is not essential but fun motoring.

Back Axle and Gearbox. It is worth getting expert advice over back axle ratios. You often have a choice and should go for one which will give you a swift bus-like speed rather than one suitable for a slug-like tipper. A five-speed gearbox which can often be fitted in standard models gives you greater flexibility and is ideal for the mountains to come, provided the gears are evenly spaced.

Compression. Get advice over engine compression. If you buy a second-hand, petrol-engined camper, be sure it has not got a high compression engine – petrol is often very low octane – see Chapter 9.

Suspension. Generally, stock campers have poor suspension and are uncomfortable on some continental and eastern roads and therefore exhausting. You should test vehicles and seek authoritative advice. I think the answer lies perhaps in improving what you have to buy by going for larger wheels, outsize tyres if the steering will take it and heavier shock absorbers. Small wheels and a short chassis do make a car wallow.

Volkswagen microbus conversions have easy suspension, but I think due to this smoothness, are driven too fast. Independent suspension is easy on *your* bottom but the shocks still go on at the *car's* bottom and I have seen many VWs with suspension trouble on the way. The hare did not win, you know.

Clearance. Choose a vehicle with a good clearance and not too much overhang.

Fuel Tank. Get as large a fuel tank as possible – you sometimes have a choice. Have an extra strap put round your fuel tank and make sure that the straps are all packed with some material to break the shocks of the road. I once looked out of the window when breakfasting with a friend en route and saw one of the two straps on my tank hanging down on the ground. I had nearly lost my fuel and it was Mutt's luck as usual that we were at one of the Pakistan Tobacco Factories where the resident mechanics patched up the strap for me until I could get a third one put on at the end of my journey in Delhi. You don't need an extra tank fitted – there are so many petrol stations, but a large tank saves frequent halts.

Tyres. I favour Michelin steel-braced radial tyres which have done me extremely well and seldom puncture. Your dealer can give you the correct tyre pressure if you get your loaded vehicle weighed first.

With double back wheels, see that you can get your foot-pump on to both valves. They can be awkward to get at and may need modification. Try your pump out before starting – you can't get compressed air in the middle of a desert. Be sure you have a jack and take a couple of tyre levers in case of a puncture. Roadside garages do not always have them.

Seats. Bostrom slim-line shock-absorbing seats or a similar make will soften your ride if the standard ones need improving. Your seats should provide you with an upright position which is the least indigestion-producing for long hours and bumpy roads. Seat belts are of course mandatory and I prefer the recoil type. The others can rub you badly motoring day after day and are too confining.

Mirrors and Horns. I will mention the importance of good mirrors and horns in Chapter 9. You want horns which will wake the dead, as well as your standard one.

Lights. Some people advocate extra-strong headlights, but if you do install them, see that your wiring will take them. If you up-gun you must up-wire. In the east lorries seldom have dippers. For them it is all or side. Therefore it is better not to initiate a Brocks' benefit, but to drive with your heads dipped and two spotlights on a separate switch, mounted low and beamed wide to pick out both edges of the road some sixty yards ahead, and the minor users such as bullock and buffalo carts whose drivers will be asleep anyway.

Headlamps and spotlights should have chrome net screens. Until I installed them I invariably had one or more of these cracked by flying stones and gravel thrown up by oncoming traffic.

Flashers and Washers. These are generally standard, but should be fitted if not. (I will stress the importance of flashers in Chapter 9.) One does often meet rain and lorries throw up a lot of mud.

Fire Extinguisher. Have this mounted in the cab, easily got at in case of need.

Towing Rings. Have towing rings fitted to the front direct on to the main chassis members, not the bumpers. Don't have them on the back. If you do, someone will persuade you to tow *him*.

7. *The Living Quarters*

Through Cabs, Windows, Ventilation, Insulation and Heating, Colour, Interior Walls and Furniture, Lighting and Batteries, Cooking, Gas, Fridges, Water, WC's, Loading.

Stock campers could be better designed for our purposes. Most assume that every day will be a warm summer's day in a temperate climate. They are full of gadgets which tend to go wrong as vibration plays havoc with them and it will spoil your holiday if the apple of your eye develops blights. You can, however, improve the design. Equally, you can adopt such improvements if designing for yourself.

Through Cabs. Most vehicles have a through-cab for space. This allows a lot of foul dust to get in to the living quarters that has to be cleaned out before you can settle in for the night. Sliding doors are expensive to fit, but a heavy curtain is a help and helps to keep you warm. If building for yourself, consider having a box body separate from the cab with screw-down windows, if the chassis is big enough.

Windows. Most campers have too much glass window for privacy or warmth and skimpy cotton curtains. Indians, for instance, are particularly quizzy. They mean no harm, but are gregarious and like to crowd up. You can fit venetian blinds for privacy and thick curtains. The latter ensure that you do not show lights when camping wild. All this cuts down condensation, the camper's bugbear.

Ventilation. If you are building for yourself, do not put in a roof ventilator. It is an inherent weakness. You will always get some blithe spirit who will signal you on – 'Lots of room overhead old boy' – and crunch! You then have a very large hole in your roof – the worst possible place. I have known instances where the ventilator has been laboriously unscrewed and valuables removed. If you have one already, see if you can fit in a grid for security and a dark cover for night-time. Otherwise I suggest a high-up, small side window above your stove and a hit and miss ventilator low down somewhere to make a through current of air.

Insulation and Heating. Pay great attention to insulation (generally neglected) and put in more yourself if necessary. There are many forms of polyurethane that can be easily applied. I use polystyrene under a facing of vinylized plywood, but that is a big carpentering job.

In a properly insulated vehicle your lights and your own body heat will warm the place up quickly, even in frosty conditions. If you can plug in to the mains in a permanent camp, you can use a table lamp and small stove as well. Lack of insulation encourages condensation and everything will remain damp until, on leaving Europe, you begin to see real sun and have a dry out. Insulation against cold is insulation against heat too. The unmodified week-end camper is like a baking tin in the heat, and at the opposite extreme, a gas fire consumes fuel and needs a lot of ventilation.

To increase the warmth at night you can fit cut-outs of say, expanded polyurethane over those windows not used for air. I do this myself and they have the added advantage of cutting down exterior noise and light – useful in a crowded camp or lorry park.

Colour. A white roof makes for coolness. If you have a choice, choose a bright colour for the body. Subdued or mist-coloured campers do not show up when driving.

Interior Walls and Furniture. If you are building for yourself have these entirely washable. If you cannot get P.V.C. covers for seats and mattresses get removable stretch covers that can be washed. One cannot entirely keep out dirt. If there is a carpet, see if you can replace it with vinyl tiles, shiny surfaced for easy cleaning. Incidentally have your floor in one piece if possible. A plank floor tends to work while the vehicle is moving and crack tiles, etc.

Floor to ceiling cupboards are good design as they help to brace the body too and do not go against the principle of keeping weight low if you put light stuff in the upper shelves. In all cases put strong bolts and catches on all doors if they are not already there. Otherwise movement will burst the doors open and deposit everything on the floor. A height of 3ft. 6in. is enough for a hanging cupboard whose contents seem to weigh a ton. Your clothes should travel in hanging plastic bags with zip fasteners, or they will rub into holes.

Try for a camper whose furniture is deployable in a few easy movements. Some designs seem to require a sort of general post when setting up beds and tables and the smaller the vehicle, the greater the movement of possessions. You don't want to spend hours settling in at the end of a tiring day.

Those folding beds used for seats by day can stick and always seem to have hard, biscuit-thin mattresses. A very comfortable mattress is essential. Remember, you may have been driving for a long time. If your camper is small, lightly inflated Lilos can solve the problem.

Lighting and Batteries. Most campers have fluorescent lighting. It is economic in power once the gas-filled tubes are warmed up, but to do this takes a fairly strong initial boost of current. Don't keep switching them on and off. Decide how many you need and keep them on until the final 'lights out'. Better still, have lights on the table or wall which plug in to the mains as an alternative in a camp.

When you are not travelling it is unnecessary to charge your batteries by static running. Plug in to the mains and clip on a little converter to the batteries. Converters are very reliable and quite cheap. Insist on a heavy-duty battery and if possible install a second one linked to it. Carry a hydrometer to test them. When camping wild for some days in one place you may need a generator. There are good ones on the market weighing only a few pounds.

Cooking. Characteristically, makers of stock campers in England fit in gas cookers with absurdly small cylinders. Yet they also supply fridges and water heaters which consume gas from these same cylinders, at a great rate. Therefore, get the largest cylinders you can carry. Butane (Camping Gaz) is the most common abroad and two 22lb cylinders would seem to be a sensible size. On a winter trip a ventilated cupboard is as useful as a fridge is and one can heat up water in a big kettle and save all that fuel needed for a water heater. Seek advice about cylinder storage and learn the proper routine for turning off gas, otherwise collected escaped gas may cause an explosion.

Gas can be got quite easily in Turkey and Iran, but not without difficulty in Afghanistan. Pakistan has her own excellent supplies from

Sui in Baluchistan piped all over the country. It is a kind of butane. Gas can only be got in India in large cities such as Delhi, Bombay, Calcutta and Madras from the depots of the major oil companies such as Burma, Shell and Indianoil. The depots in Delhi are three or four miles out from the Ring Road along the Rohtak Road.

If building for yourself make your galley embrasure heatproof. I am not personally in favour of ovens. Your wife or cook might as well not have a holiday since they force elaborate and fuel consuming cooking on her/him. If you are a sybarite, go and have a delicately flavoured Mughal or Kashmiri meal occasionally. If you are set on savouring the east, have a Madras prawn curry with all the fixings. If you do, you may blow a gasket, but you'll feel startled into freshness. The old guard actually start sweating in anticipation.

A pressure cooker is a 'must'. It can reduce stringy mutton (generally goat in disguise) and ropy chicken into edibility, is quick for all types of cooking, and easy to use outside (see Chapters 10, 11 and Appendix I).

Fridges. I cast doubts above on the importance of fridges. Apart from their greed for fuel they should be absolutely level when running on gas. Most fridge owners carry spirit levels with them, but it is very difficult to find somewhere absolutely flat to park in the rather makeshift camps beyond Turkey. A fridge can easily be put out of action by vibration and is not easy to repair abroad. At a firm base camp you can often get a container full of ice. Unless you are trying to develop ulcers you don't want frigid drinks in the winter. Bourbon on the rocks can get you on the rocks too.

Water. Most campers carry vast containers of water – a heavy, unnecessary burden, that is often laborious to fill up. If you have big tanks, consider removing them and using the space more usefully. Two portable, two-gallon jerricans stored low down are quite enough for four people. We find consumption for all purposes is half a gallon each per day and one can get water easily all the way. See p. 77 for water purifying.

W.Cs. To have a W.C. or not to have a W.C.? That is the question. I like to get down to basic principles in this. Don't take with you that which is best left behind. However soil is neutralized, fluid has to be carried and anyway the whole idea is revolting. A portable W.C. is space consuming, especially in a small camper. There are facilities the whole way through. As you go east they are often of the eastern style and you will find them very smelly. One gets used to them quickly: the sense of smell is easily fatigued. In an emergency en route or in a lone camp, you can walk off into the scrub with a detached air, bearing a good trowel. One can always have some sort of temporary arrangement inside the vehicle if stuck in a crowded place while having repairs done and so on.

One always meets the unexpected in India. A wealthy Parsi told me she had installed flush W.Cs. in her house including one for her driver's quarters. He always neglected to flush after use. This was because to do so would have been beneath his caste and was the job of an untouchable!

Loading. If you have to put baggage on the roof, your vehicle is too small for you or you have too much baggage: the artist is known by what he omits. It is the worst place in which to put weight, since it acts as a sort of lever. Your tyre walls will ache and your suspension too. You will create dangerous instability, the more you pile on. Roof gear is easily pilfered. The corollary is, don't have a roof rack – keep out of temptation.

If you are building for yourself you can have locking devices for jerri-cans, but why put them on the roof? Attach them to the members in trays or in compartments inside the skirt with budget locks.

All this really boils down to simplicity and strength. You don't want to be fiddling about with bits and pieces all day, or always mending things as they fall apart.

8. *Servicing and Spares*

SERVICING – Agents, Oiling and Greasing, Running Repairs. SPARES – Keys, Tools, Plugs, Diesel Injectors, Fuel Pumps and Filter Cartridges, Electrical, Gaskets and Oil Filters, The Cooling System, Dipstick and Filler Caps, Liquid Stores, Lick and Stick, Tyres, Oil Can and Grease Gun, Towing Strap.

SERVICING

Agents. In your choice of vehicle you must of course take account of the servicing and availability of large spares en route for that make. I would suggest getting a list of agents outside Europe for your make of vehicle from the suppliers before you start. There is fair coverage for English makes as far as Afghanistan, particularly in Ankara and Teheran, though foreign cars such as VWs are far better served. There is little coverage in Afghanistan as the cars are largely Russian. Import restrictions make things difficult in Pakistan and India, but the mechanics of both countries are very skilled at improvization.

Oiling and Greasing. One can get this done at many service stations run by the big oil companies in Greece, Turkey, Pakistan and India. There are also large service stations in Teheran.

Running Repairs. Every good-sized town in Turkey onwards has a number of small workshops on the outskirts, each expertly specializing in one single aspect of repairs. The standard of work in Iran and Pakistan is very high indeed.

If you have to footslog it for great distances to get help in a breakdown, don't do it in the middle of the day. Be comforted, the combustion engine can generally be coaxed to get you to some haven of rescue, even if, as is unlikely no one appears out of the blue to help you. A Turkish gorilla dived into my engine and upset my two Weber carburettors before I could stop him with a rugby tackle. This was most annoying as it was in one of the few countries where neither of us speaks the language. We had real trouble eight hundred miles later in the back of beyond as he'd put the whole engine out of tune. I was wrestling with little success as it needs special knowledge. It is too, quite impossible if, like me, you are slightly deaf from war's percussions and there is a constant roar from passing juggernauts and Turkish 'advisers'. I was beginning to blow my top when a voice with a foreign accent said, 'Can I help you?'

I said, 'No, it's hopeless! These —— Weber carburettors are out of tune. I was a silly mug ever to fit them.'

'Weber!' he cried. '*I* am Weber!'

He was just that – the only Weber expert for thousands of miles on his way home from a holiday in Pakistan. He tuned the carburettors as well as anyone can with no special instruments. We gave him a bottle of Harvey's Bristol Cream (our future Xmas celebration tipple), further cementing the Entente Cordiale – Inshallah! (By the will of Allah).

SPARES

The decision as to what spares to take with you is a difficult one. The age of the vehicle has a bearing on this problem. However many you take, you may well find that you haven't the one you need in an emergency. If you ask the maker or agents what you are likely to need, you will probably get a silly answer. When I asked a well-known maker to give me a short list of the spares to replace parts that most commonly go wrong, it was so long that I realized it would mean that I would have to be followed by two large trucks bearing the spares. Either they were very pushing salesmen, or they had little faith in their product.

Some agents will give you a small pack on a use or return basis. The best place for spares of all types and makes en route is Teheran – at a price.

Keys. One of the most important precautions you should take is to have spare keys hidden in the engine and living quarters. One would look silly locking oneself out on a snowy mountain.

Tools. Take good tools with you and make sure that you have a spanner to fit every nut in your type of vehicle, especially if you buy it second-hand. The older English cars invariably have a few nuts that no metric tool will fit, so foreign garages will be little help if you forget a tool of the vital size. A complete set of open spanners is almost a must. Be sure that one fits the sump nut and if you have a radiator drain plug of the nut type, see that you have one that fits that too. Beware of the gorilla who advances on your car with a huge plumber's spanner – all force, but too much play. With this he'll strip any nut, especially those butter-hard brass ones. Use only a spanner that fits exactly. Remember, though, that you can file new flats on stripped nuts or bolt heads so that one of your tools will grip them.

A box spanner and tommy bar are good members of your tool box and a few long-armed ring spanners. A set of those excellent spanners in all sizes which clip on to ratchet arms is quick to operate, especially if it includes one for fitting over a plug. A gorilla in a garage has prob-ably put in your plugs anyway. Oil the thread of everything you screw in. It is easy to crack a plug if you don't exert even pressure.

Remember this gorilla I've been talking about comes sometimes from a country which finds tools hard to get. He's a gorilla with a pouch. He'll pocket your tools or leave them balanced on the engine to fall off later. Count your tools and ward off gorillas.

Plugs. I suggest you take at least one spare set of plugs for a protracted India run, but it is best to work it out for yourself. Your plugs with the characteristic bad petrol will often last you for no more than 6,000 miles. Take one or two more than you estimated, if you let gorillas near your car.

Diesel Injectors, Fuel Pumps and Filter Cartridges. If you have a diesel it may be wise to have a set of spare injectors. My diesels seemed to be rough on the fuel pump too. Take spare filter cartridges. If you have the hot plug type of starter, take spare hot plugs. Apart from this find out from other owners what can go wrong. Be sure you know how to bleed air bubbles from the fuel system. Support fuel lines when opening them, if you must, but leave sleeping lines be as much as you can. Diesels can have obstinate air leaks totally unnoticed by your dealer, though by and large, they can be very reliable if you are a lucky owner. A friend of mine did thousands of miles with a little diesel which was even more gutless than its kind generally is, only to find out at long last that it had air in the engine which required simple bleeding. No one at the suppliers discovered it, in spite of his complaining of poor performance.

Electrical. In general and especially if you have a petrol engine, take the smaller electrical spares several times over. This includes a selection of car bulbs and fluorescent tubes for the camper. They are not heavy.

Consider having an entirely duplicated coil arrangement in a cool place away from the engine. Most coils (bobbines abroad) are very close to a hot engine. Get all the advice you can over these arrangements. There are many devices which if added to your set-up can make it less liable to pack up in bad conditions. If you don't know how to change points and condensors, learn quickly. They are badly made, like all small parts these days and tend to suffer in extremes of climate, dust, etc. On the other hand if you are a lucky type, they may last for years, but don't chance it.

One heavy electrical spare you should take if you can afford it is an alternator. They can be most unreliable. Consider replacing your alternator with a heavy duty dynamo before you start and take advice on this.

Take a set of electrical screwdrivers as well as your ordinary ones. They do get lost, even on your immaculate quafila (camel train), O Brother!

Gaskets and Oil Filters. A full set of spare gaskets can be invaluable. They don't weigh much. Stiffen the packet to prevent buckling or keep it always on a flat floor. Spare oil filters are light too, so take enough for the journey. The right sizes may be scarce en route.

The Cooling System. You should have at least one spare fan belt or set of belts if you have that type of engine. They don't weigh much either. Don't forget a spare thermostat – they can go wrong.

I always fit new hoses for the radiator system, even to the thinner heater ones, at the beginning of a journey. The original ones, having been cast rather prematurely, then become my spares. Garages never tighten hose clips and often set them up so that the screw head is difficult to reach. Tighten them half a turn if you think they are loose, especially if you have just added anti-freeze. After a bit of running-in, turn the screws a bit more, but never too much. Don't be a gorilla! Garages do tighten things too much by using power tools improperly adjusted. A low hose which comes adrift can leave you with a very hot engine by the time you have extricated yourself from traffic. Need I say, this too has happened to Joe Mutt.

Dipstick and Filler Caps. Take a spare dipstick. Dipping is generally done in the rosy dawn when one is no brighter than a mud fairy. It's so easy to leave it on a rock or balance it on the engine to fall off somewhere. If you have to let go of it, put it on your seat on a cloth, together with the radiator filler cap which you have taken off to check the water level. Remember that it's part of the water pressurization, so have a twin brother in your spares kit. If dipstick and filler cap are on your seat they'll remind you about themselves. If you lose your little ewe-dipstick you won't have a clue what your oil level is for perhaps thousands of miles.

Have a spare oil filler cap too. Joe Mutt once lost one, but my wife's facecream lid fitted a treat.

Liquid Stores. Plastic rather than glass containers for distilled water, brake fluid etc. are best. This rule also applies to stores, especially of the liquid type. Have enough engine oil for topping up during the journey. You cannot carry enough for your oil changes which you can get anyway in the larger centres, but it saves a lot of bother if you don't have to go out prospecting when you stop in the desert. Take small plastic bottles of the other oils (gearbox, steering box, rear axle etc.) with attached filler pipes. These oils are often difficult to get in India.

Lick and Stick. I always take malleable binding wire. I prefer tape of the medical bandage type to that flat black insulation tape, but now a plastic one (Dencon) is on the market which is very good. It is amazing what uses you can find for the first type. Elastoplast bandage soaked in Araldite can make you a replacement for a T-shaped rubber breather joint. I've actually done it, after a gorilla had torn my original one.

Tyres. Tyres are the feet of your car and therefore very important. If you don't take care of them, your expedition may become a bootless one. You should have a good pump and pressure gauge. Check the pressure before running for the day. To do so during the run would be meaningless as your pressure will go up a great deal, especially in desert heat.

If you have large wheels, one spare outer cover should be enough. If your wheels are small, you might need more but a new set of Michelin radials should do the round trip. Except in Teheran, spares are difficult to get and expensive.

You should have two or three spare inner tubes. They are neither bulky or heavy. Take a few spare tyre valves as well as spring and other washers.

Oil Can and Grease Gun. An oil can with a good spout is invaluable, but it must have a stopper or the oil will get mixed up with everything. I am taking it for granted that you have an efficient grease gun for your prop shaft.

Towing Strap. Get one of those nylon towing straps. They're not heavy and you might have to be towed one day. Joe Mutt has been, for hundreds of miles. These straps are elastic and it is much easier to follow the tower without charging him every time he stops or slows.

I hope that you will yourself ensure as far as is humanly possible that things don't go wrong and that you do not rely on others. In many garages a sick car or one which can be rendered sick in due course is far more profitable than a car that habitually gives no trouble. There is, however, a great deal of luck involved. I know of two cars, as near identical as cars can be and of the same approximate issue. One always broke down within fifteen miles of home. The other, flogged round like an eastern donkey in places where a jeep would weep, never had any trouble. A breakdown is not the end of the world; you will generally get your vehicle through, so don't be put off. Someone will help you. Take a red triangle with you, though!

9. *Driving Techniques and Conditions*

Gradients, Road Surfaces, Driving Techniques, Right-Hand Drive and Mirrors, Accidents, Stone Throwing, Floods, Altitude, Cold, Heat, Fuel, Maps.

Gradients. To give you some idea of the steepness of the roads, that is the main ones you will meet on the journey, Snowdon would be an unmarked foothill, jostled by bigger unmarked foothills. You can meet passes of up to 9,000 ft. on some routes and you cannot avoid ones of 8,500 ft. whichever way you go. Besides who wants to? It's exciting motoring.

East of Ankara you motor for hundreds of miles in Turkey at an average of 4,000 ft. and it will be steep up and down all the way. In Iran, as you return home, you can go from below sea level on the Caspian to nearly 9,000 ft., depending on which pass you take and all within forty miles, while in Afghanistan the pass above Ghazni is over 9,000 ft. You can get over these passes in any vehicle which is reasonably sound, but you may have to crawl in very low gear. Do not be put off by the engine howling. It is happier, even if you are not, than if you try to hang on to a higher gear too long. To do so might really impose too much strain on the transmission. It is, however, more fun to have a more powerful engine if you can afford it and less of an anxiety.

Road Surfaces. I have done something like sixty years' motoring – rough motoring – in the east. As a child I remember my father having a T-model Ford in Central India where the going was very rough indeed. His driver once got the car back by stuffing a punctured tyre with grass. He poured it all out in a sort of green soup when they got home.

As a young Indian Army Officer I used to set off into the blue in an open American tourer. How well and toughly they made them then. They were not the puffed-up and baked variety with marshmallow springs which bang their bottoms when off the main roads in the east today.

Later I was seconded to the Transborder Armed Police or Scouts in tribal territory beyond the North West Frontier, under a loose British administration in what is now Pakistan. The administration was rather skilfully carried out by the usual very small cadre, backed by a system of Danegeld to tribal leaders in return for keeping the peace. When this failed, the Scouts would be sent out on a punitive column. If things then got out of hand, the regular army would be called in too – the old stick and carrot. The roads were rough and apart from potholes one had to keep an eye open for home-made mines. I used to let the local buses go first on these occasions, but not out of politeness.

At one time I was Military Attaché at our Embassy in Kabul, Afghanistan. Then there were unbelievably rough scrape roads. A scrape road is the next grade down from a Macadam road. It is formed by mounting a scraper blade on a bulldozer which pushes the blade along the desert to 'scrape' a road. There are generally drainage ditches on both sides. The desert is mostly stony, but where sand is encountered, donkey loads of shingle are brought up to give the road more foundation. The fact that the blade judders as it is pushed forward causes corrugation from the outset. These corrugations get deeper as they weather. If the bulldozer hasn't been past recently, you can be shaken to a jelly. The same technique is used over mountain roads, which generally have a bit more in the way of foundations.

I remember being part of a motorcade, all dolled up as I was with 'chicken guts', as we called our aiguillettes, suspended from one shoulder to meet the king returning from abroad – a normal official ceremony. We followed the French Ambassador in his huge American car which got up such a rhythmic bounce that the chauffeur had to stop and lean on the vehicle until the heaves subsided. His Excellency, not unnaturally, had turned the colour of a crème de menthe frappée.

My official car was one of those knocked-together ones that one got just after the war. It was under-engined even without my bulk, so boiled immediately in the hotter parts of the country if there were a following, rear-quarter or side wind. The buna (artificial rubber) tyres punctured readily, but the vibration of the corrugated roads was so fierce that we never discovered the disaster until a normal stop was made. By then the inner tube came out in pieces no larger than bits of a jig-saw puzzle.

When we first did this trip, some thirteen years ago, the roads were scrape all the way from Ankara eastwards and it was adventure in the raw. One used the steering wheel as a lifebelt to hold on to in order to stay in position. The passenger hit the roof as a matter of course. The roads have now got progressively better and are collectively known as the Asian Highway, for which, as I have said, one no longer needs four-wheel drive. One now starts talking breezily about driving over to India for the winter. But beware of *hubris*, retribution is always just round the corner and you must expect the unexpected. Often a sudden fold in the road is concealed by shadow and as it hurls you upwards you can't damp down with the brakes. Nemesis may always strike on roads where opportunism and disregard for good driving manners are the rule.

Nowadays there is tarmac, often of a rather crumby (non-skid) type through most of Turkey, except over the highest passes where frost damage makes the maintenance of a good surface impossible. Nearing the Iranian border, although the road is tarred, it is very narrow and cut up by container lorries. Poverty, winter conditions and the weight of traffic have so far prevented improvement.

From the Iranian border onwards the road is excellent throughout your journey in Iran. New roads are being built everywhere. Prosperity appears to follow the roads, cotton ginning and sugar-beet refining factories seeming to spring up like mushrooms. In the last ten years water has been brought to the deserts by pipe and artesian wells so that agricultural development has sprouted quickly, served by the new roads. Motor transport runs freely where so much of it before was in repair shops, knocked to pieces by potholes. It used to take us four days' hard driving to get from the border to Teheran. Now we take a leisurely one and a half.

Don't, however, get over-confident. Much of the country is part or wholly desert with a soil-erosion problem. Mountain rains don't get sopped up by vegetation and a modern bridge can be occasionally broken by a raging yellow flood. Beware of dangerous crosswinds as you come round mountain corners. Side valleys will suddenly funnel a concentrated gust at you like a punch. I saw a huge Benz bus (they do about ninety miles an hour to all other traffic's discomfiture) lying on its roof in the fairway. It must have taken off on a gust and turned nose over tail.

In Afghanistan the roads are either concrete slab (Russian) or tarmac (American) and well maintained.

In Pakistan and India roads are never very good and mostly very bad, although many are tarred. These are big countries and the monsoons are damaging, so it is small blame to them. It is no mean feat to keep up communications at all on a small budget. Nearly all the roads are hand-made. That means that round river boulders are broken up laboriously into chippings beside the road that is to be rebuilt and warm tar is spread over it from watering cans and smoothed out by hand. Little effort is made to get down to more solid foundations. Modern plant is only just beginning to appear.

Driving Techniques. Once you leave Europe, you are in a diesel world. The drivers of diesels are winders-up and hate reducing speed. By this I mean that a diesel takes far longer to reach a high speed than a petrol engine, lacking acceleration particularly in the earlier stages. Having at last reached a good speed, the driver is reluctant to slow down again. Even if yours is the right of way, he will compete for the gap. If you have a flasher – which is a 'must' – and if you flash first, claiming your right, nine times out of ten he will concede. But look out for the tenth and don't be caught out in England where a flash, if it means anything, means – After you, Sir. On returning to the U.K. I was being crowded on my side by one of those Granadas, all spare tin squared-off. I flashed as I thought, to claim my right, upon which the Granada pushed through, its driver bowing sweetly in acknowledgement as I stood on my nose to avoid him.

Eastern drivers, not having been at it so long, have not generally learned to give and take, which as we have learnt, is the smoothest and safest way. They are all aggressive and opportunist. If you are considerately polite in a lawless maelstrom like Istamboul or Teheran, you will get nowhere. The gap that opens will be seized by crossing traffic. Above all, keep the initiative. Make gaps by edging forward, but always be in instant control down to an inch. Use a small horn to twitter as much as is needed to be heard above the general noise and when necessary a 'Gerrout' with big horns, even in the main avenues. Then and only then will they admit that you are a better man than they, or at least nearly as good. You get the knack of it in time and actually enjoy it. It is of course harder with a diesel as it hasn't the acceleration to leap into a gap.

In this aggressive world always expect the unexpected. If you on the main road see a bigger vehicle converging from a side one, do not assume he'll let you pass. He will enter the main road without a check.

You get the downhill Charlies too who overrun their engines. They are hard to shake off and sometimes don't want to be shaken off. With good gear changes and a gearbox suited to certain gradients you may pass them with ease uphill. Then you will save your brakes going downhill, only to have Charlie scream past. This may go on for a long time. Pause, and let the lunatic go.

Downhills are steep and long, after seemingly endless climbs, so save your brakes. Get into a suitably low gear at once and only dab your brakes from time to time. Dabbing keeps them cooler than applying them for a period, however lightly. Trucks have emergency working handbrakes on the transmission, which means that they have a second cold brake in time of trouble. I found this a great comfort in my last camper which was based on a truck chassis.

Right-hand Drive and Mirrors. Remember you switch to the right of the road on reaching Calais (where the east starts) and you don't return to the 'correct' side of the road until crossing into Pakistan, and so continue throughout India. If you have a right-hand drive, have exceptionally good mirrors, especially on the left side. You can get split ones for close and far vision. Carry spares. You will get them nicked off by oncoming traffic on a bend. So far I've never had a scrape, but have had mirrors plucked off.

Once, one of those maniacal bus drivers who cavort at a hideous speed all over Turkey and Iran and who are both the kings and bullies of the road, overtook me and to show off skimmed too close and whipped off my mirror. I put on my 'Gerrout' horn so persistently that it unnerved him and he stopped. I was so angry that I was getting ready with one of those that start almost at ground level; when out stepped an absolute Primo Carnera. I confined myself to abuse in which I regretted in a pitying way that he had only a mother.

Turkish buses have names like Thunderbolt, Lightning and By the Will of Allah (God Help Us!), so don't say you haven't been warned.

Accidents. Pedestrians are as unpredictable in the country as in the towns. Some upland peasant may see a friend on the other side of the road and dart across without a glance. He comes to a village perhaps once a month to swap a skeletal chicken for a second-hand cap. He's not used to traffic. It would go very ill for you should you hit him, so just take it slow and you'll be all right. In Turkey and Iran although attitudes are friendly, should you have a bump you are automatically assumed to be at fault. The reasoning is that you are extra to the normal traffic and the accident would not have happened had you not been there. Whatever the situation, it is wiser not to stop on the spot, but to report to the nearest police station. Crowds can turn very ugly.

Stone Throwing. I advised you above to go slowly through villages, but from Turkey onwards small boys and girls frequently throw quite large stones at foreign cars and campers. Their intent appears to be to break a windscreen or, in parts of Turkey, blackmail drivers into giving them cigarettes. In any case shepherds hate cars. One must be constantly on the look-out and the temptation to speed up is great. If you see a child stoop, slow up and point at it, with your loud horns blaring. In most cases it will drop the stone and run, or at the worst you will take the stone behind rather than on your windscreen, where a protective net would be cumbersome.

Floods. If there is a flood across the road after a rainstorm always walk across the breach first when the water is subsiding, and you think it safe to take your vehicle through. There may be a hole under the opaque waters which might smash your camper, or a big boulder may have been rolled down by the flood. Having got a good line, never stall your engine or water will come up the exhaust. Always take water slowly or you'll drown your electrics. Some people take off the fan belt to stop the fan scooping water over the plugs. Personally, I'd rather wait a bit, though waiting is not in my nature.

Never, never listen to spectators who wave you on and assure you that the bottom is smooth, hard and in shallow water. They are hanging about for the fun of seeing you, a 'Have', provide free entertainment for the 'Have-Nots'. In any case there is always a chance of getting a reward for helping you out. A friend of mine was persuaded into the flood and plunged in like Horatius in the spirit of 'Take thou in charge this day'. He stuck and the vulture-like squatters on the bank pulled him out backwards, but also pulled his fibreglass body in half. He was held up for a month for repairs.

Altitude. Very generally speaking, the higher you go above sea level the more poorly your engine performs. This applies to both diesel and petrol, though some of the former have fuel richness controls to effect a moderate improvement. The whole problem of upland motoring in a dry rarified atmosphere needs, I feel, research beyond the scope of this book. The following phenomenon can, however, be disturbing for the beginner.

I have found that my three campers in succession, two diesel and one petrol, all suffered quite unnervingly at certain points on the route to India. So well do I know the way that I can identify the very milestone where all three cars have started to pull very badly. This is at about 5,000 ft. in an airless re-entrant (blind valley) where there is no vegetation, near Ab Ali between Teheran and the Caspian. The temperature at the time is generally mild, so I put it down to lack of oxygen with no plant life to create it or breeze to feed in fresh air. When I get out on the higher spurs above 6,000 ft., all three engines have picked up merrily, although as I crane my neck out awkwardly at the 5,000 ft. mark to look up almost vertically at tight horseshoe after tight horseshoe with large container lorries looking no bigger than black flies on a stalk, my experienced heart quails a bit. How much more will that of a beginner. I round on my poor navigator and wail, 'The blasted car will never make it. I'll turn it in as scrap at the next village' – sure signs that the captain's morale is at its highest ebb, as a Pakistani military instructor once said. But be comforted, keep down in a low gear and potter up. It's surprising how soon the vast crags above pass below your wheels.

Cold. Even in spring and autumn – the best times to travel in the uplands – there is the chance of frost damage. Insulation is, as I said in Chapter 7, vital. Of course, you will have anti-freeze in your radiator. It should be put in in the same proportions as you would use in England since your drive will not always be very cold. A radiator muff with graduated openings is a good thing, but watch your temperature gauge, as you can suddenly overheat if it's kept on too long. That said, it is invaluable in the early morning before the sun is up. I make my own muff out of P.V.C. Should you travel in mid-winter – if you must for it's a risky ordeal – you might be wise to have a miner's lamp suspended near your carburettor and fuel lines at night. This creates a warm area under the bonnet which will prevent the engine oil from becoming too stiff with cold for the engine to turn over easily. A flat miner's lamp under the sump would help too. Diesel fuel is especially affected by cold. Erzerum is exposed and Joe Mutt once had to beam a Tilley stove on to the diesel fuel lines for two hours there before the engine would start.

Heat. You may get a very hot dry following wind in the rarified air of the uplands in warmer seasons. If so, watch your temperature gauge like a hawk and cruise more slowly in the heat to keep the temperature down. If it starts rising, switch on your car heater. You may have to roast, but the engine will cool off a bit. You may find too that if you have an overdrive, the fan does not supply sufficient draught. If so, change to the next gear down. Failing this, stop and cool down with the engine turning over faster than a mere tick-over. At this point, I would remove the thermostat from the cooling system. It's a dangerous little thing. I once had one that suddenly jammed in the closed position and I lost an engine in a hot, following wind in an instantaneous overheat. The local desert truck drivers never use thermostats, but you may find your camper can cope without these precautions, or the wind may be a head one.

I find that a car runs hotter with anti-freeze. This is a firm opinion I have formed with all vehicles I have driven. No one can give me the reason. So, if you take the thermostat out, you might take the antifreeze out too, but if so, don't throw it away. If it is too bulky to take with you, leave it with someone reliable to be collected on your return, as it is hard to get in Pakistan and India, where it is not necessary in any case.

You should put your thermostat back when normal conditions return as your engine will run better.

If you overheat with loss of water, *never* top up with cold water with the engine switched off. You'll crack the cylinder head. Stop and wait for the engine to cool off before refilling slowly with the engine running. If you are in a hurry, why not heat up water on your kitchen stove for re-filling?

Do not deflate your tyres for hot desert stretches. It may make them hotter through having more surface touching the road and thereby increasing friction. If you are in doubt about crossing the deserts in the hot weather when blow-outs are more likely, travel in the evening and early night or morning. The small hours can be dangerous and ambushes are not unknown. They are unlikely while local trucks are still plying during the early part of the night.

Fuel. People travelling for the first time are often anxious about getting fuel in the remoter countries. Petrol, diesel and engine oil are available along the main routes at fifty mile intervals or less. Very rarely, one or more stations may be empty, so you would be wise to carry spare jerricans in order to have a reserve should you expect to be unlucky.

Jerricans are most useful if you have a petrol vehicle whose engine cannot digest the local brew. Often, particularly in Turkey at the moment, Normal petrol is very bad. It starts off at about 80 octane only and may well be adulterated. It would pay you to use Super when you can get it – I will indicate the stations in the route chapters – and carry some to mix with Normal when you can't. Super starts off at about 93 octane – near our two-star. I have found that BP and Shell are more reliable in Turkey than local brands.

In Iran, the petrol is all of local production and nowadays quite good. Normal is about 88 octane and super 93. In Afghanistan, some stations claim to have two grades. Go for the one they say is best. The cost is the same, but it is probably the one used by town dignitaries and could even be 80 octane. As far as Kandahar the petrol comes from Iran, but after that as far as the Pakistan border it will be Russian and much worse. Keep some of your Iranian super for this stretch unless your car has a most unusual digestion. The Russian will be rough on your plugs anyway and it smells like tramps' socks.

In Pakistan and India petrol is readily obtainable at the same intervals of about fifty miles. Normal is about 86 and super 93 octane. Super is quite easy to find in Pakistan, but in India only in the larger cities.

Diesel is everywhere of reasonable quality.

Maps. Travel without maps is like eggs without salt – to paraphrase Kipling. The Bartholomew World Travel Series is sufficiently up-to-date to be useful, but over-optimistic about roads in West Pakistan, between Multan and Quetta. These maps show the relief of the terrain – a matter of considerable interest when planning a warm night stop in cold weather.

You can get perfectly good tourist maps as you enter most countries or from Information Bureaux during your passage through them. Many of them have bureaux in London too. BP and Shell petrol stations often have maps produced by the big companies. The so-called tourist map of Afghanistan is a bit sketchy and difficult to get except in Kabul.

It is almost impossible to get good maps of India from the happy-go-lucky and unpredictable Government Tourist Bureau on the Jan Path in New Delhi. Bartholomew is your best bet there.

The English motoring organizations produce good tabulated route books and they will make out special routes for you on request. They are not always accurate as they depend for much of their information on you and me when we get home. They also supply good routes through the major towns as far as and including Teheran.

All this information is of course liable to changes. The general trend is for border crossings to become progressively simplified. The one thing that does not change is the wisdom of making one member of the expedition, *not* the driver, responsible for all documentation, finance and navigation. This saves the driver a great deal of fatigue. He can just concentrate on driving. The navigator would be wise to study the route beforehand. It is fatal to have one's head buried in a map or route book at a crucial crossroads.

10.   *Stores*

Shopping before or en Route, Bread and Butter, Flour and Biscuits, Rice and Other Cereals, Sugar and Jam, Marmite, Cooking Oil and Olive Oil, Soup, Olives, Cheese and Nuts, Yoghourt, Tinned Food, Fresh Meat and Eggs, Vegetables and Fruit, Curry, Pickles and Spices, Condiments, Sweets, Tea, Milk, Coffee, Alcohol, Soft Drinks, Vitamin Tablets. QUANTITIES.

Shopping before or en Route. The great question is whether to live off the country or, at the other extreme, take all stores and as many drinks as you are allowed with you. This boils down to a matter of economics. If you are well on in years and can afford it, have a big comfortable vehicle and take bulk stores from the U.K. Buying in bulk will offset the extra cost of fuel for a large vehicle to some extent and you avoid the bore of shopping for the duller things on your journey. If you are young and agile and can only afford a small vehicle, live off the country, but be choosy about clean food. This last applies especially if you have children. In any case, you must take any special food or medicine for them with you and enough dried milk for the journey – milk is often difficult to find while travelling and the quality may be suspect.

If you are a large party in a large vehicle or vehicles, you can carry a great deal, but don't overload – when in doubt, leave it out. There is a great temptation, first time out, to put in everything you think you might possibly need. Ten to one, you'll never use it all. Resist any urge to take the parrot and the kitchen sink – you are not a tinker.

If you can carry a lot, you can save a lot by doing your shopping in bulk in the U.K., preferably from a cash-and-carry store. These are generally kind to expeditions and our local supermarket gives us a good discount for bulk when we buy for six months at a time. I am a great believer in shopping en route for trifles of food and other items, but I am not in favour of slogging round noisy bazaars for the staples of life which could have been bought at home in bulk. Shopping is only fun if it is not a foot-wearying chore. If you speak languages or try to do so, it is even greater fun. How much you will buy to take with you depends, as I have indicated, on your circumstances and your appetites. I will make some suggestions as to quantities at the end of this chapter.

Since you can almost certainly take enough fresh food with you to see you through Europe, where food is very expensive, and enough stores for the rest of the way with the exception of fresh vegetables, fruit, bread etc., I will chiefly discuss supplies in India, where you will probably need to restock.

Bread and Butter, Flour and Biscuits. On your journey bread is very good once you have left England. One is glad to leave the flaccid, steam-cooked loaf. Bread is baked on the premises in Turkey and the sign is 'Bakker'. The loaves, usually long and crusty, are displayed in the shop window.

In Iran the bread is outstanding. It comes in three main types. One huge, thin, biscuity flap is appropriately called Fil Gush (Elephant's Ear). But then Persian is the most descriptive of all languages. Better still is the ordinary Nan (bread), generally shaped like a snowshoe and semi-leavened. You can get this in eastern Turkey too. Last of all is the Nan-in-Sangak, the bread of the little stones. It is baked on a bed of little round stones in the oven and comes out looking like strips of ribbed cork matting. It's heavenly, but before you fall upon it, see that no stones are still adhering. Always insist on Nan straight from the oven, while it is too hot for flies to settle on it. This applies too to skewered kababs at the meat stalls. Buy them flaming hot and put them in a fly-proof container or cover them. I doubt if even these precautions work in Afghanistan. The flies seem to win every time and amoebic dysentery is endemic. You should watch the Persians baking. The baker does a sort of rhythmic dance, putting in and taking bread out of the oven. He works as if possessed – and he is – by his own rhythm which makes his limbs light and tireless.

The Afghan bread is similar to the Persian but of less good quality flour and never hygienic.

You can get bread, butter, flour and biscuits in India, but have whole-meal flour ground before your eyes. This is a precaution I have taken, but it sometimes tastes musty to a western palate. If you don't see it ground, then the wheat will be mixed with inferior grains and God knows what. I take as much flour as I can with me.

Bread can present the greatest problem. Pakistan and Indian baker's bread is sweet mustiness in loaf form and if you must eat it, hard to get in remote camps. The Ashoka Hotel in New Delhi produces a good brown bread at its cake shop, but that is no use if one is not in Delhi. You should learn to make eastern prathas, chapatties and puris. Chapatties are thin, flat pancakes cooked on an iron plate. The other two are similar but cooked with butter or oil. These are made from wholemeal flour and do not need an oven – see Appendix I for recipes. They can be delicious, while prathas and puris do not need butter with them. Butter can be hard to get in India away from big cities and is not very nice as well as being expensive. You can add potatoes, spices or vegetables to prathas and make your lunch off them.

We usually start from England with enough butter to see us to our destination as well as some poly-unsaturated margarine which will keep up to three months.

Biscuits in any form are invaluable for a quick snack when bread is not available and there is no time to make it. I refer to Ryvita, Vitawheat, Krackawheat, etc. In addition, if you have space, cream or chocolate biscuits in tins are always useful, particularly with children or if you are suddenly and unexpectedly visited by just those foreign people you have come to meet. It is easy to produce tea and biscuits and an elegant thing to do in some remote place. Buy only those that are in strong tins – most of them buckle. Fruit cakes serve the same purpose and are very useful while you are driving for a quick pick-me-up. You can get sweet biscuits and plain ones in India, but like the flour they are not very nice and the packets are generally half full of paper and very expensive.

Rice and Other Cereals. I have found the same drawbacks in buying rice in India as in buying flour. Take some with you for a start and seek advice in the country. Basmati rice from the Punjab is probably the best. I once bought rice in small sacks from a leading store in New Delhi which were stamped Dehra Dun, a place as famous for rice as Patna, only to find it all musty. So I take Whitworth or Uncle Ben with me. En route, the best rice in the world comes from the Resht district of Khorassan in eastern Iran.

Another cereal, lentils or dhal, is an excellent source of protein and therefore helps out poor and expensive meat. We buy in bulk in England, but you can get it for much the same price in many different varieties in

India. It is nicest when cooked in the pressure cooker and not in the sloppy, watery way that is now the fashion in India – see Appendix I for recipe.

You can get cornflakes in India, but they are rather musty and not crisp.

Sugar and Jam. It is a good thing to take some sugar with you if you prefer it brown. One can get a coarse, unrefined type of brown sugar, known as ghur in Pakistan and India, but it is not very sweet and is usually crawling with flies.

English jam is a shade better than Indian, of which Kissan, an old-established firm, is the best. I say a shade better because I am struggling through one of those seven pound tins with a very sensible plastic lid to fit over, once it is opened. Although it is the product of a leading English firm, who allege that it is plum jam, what a mess it is. It is not jam. It is a smooth, glutinous mass that one would previously have called jelly. It is sickly sweet and has a vague plum flavour, possibly conjured up in a laboratory. So I generally stick to jam which just has to have bits of fruit in it. They can't counterfeit blackcurrant jam which is full of berries, or can they?

They have. I've just opened a tin from an even more reputable and expensive firm. The seven pound tin contains a half handful of black-currants and blatantly admits to being made of sugar, glucose syrup, pectin (turnips to you, and they form the main sludge), fruit acid (what fruit?), sodium citrate and colour. The Min. of Ag. and Fish must think that humans are ruminants and do well on turnips.

In spite of this I do stock in plenty of jam as it is easy to handle, goes well with every sort of bread and keeps well. The chunky type of mar-malade is a good bet and so is mincemeat; we take seven pound tins of them too. Mincemeat is particularly good with puris. Marmite is sup-posed to be very nutritious as well as being full of Vitamin B. It is handy with camp-made bread, but the containers are heavy.

Cooking Oil and Olive Oil. One cannot carry enough butter for the whole trip and as I said before it is often difficult to get. After eating what we have with us we depend on cooking oil for our fats. Most cooking oil in India is suspect. If you are young you will do all right on Postman (ground nut oil) or the vegetable cooking fats. Ground nut oil is not very digestible; the people who grow ground nuts in India never eat them. A vegetable oil like Dhalda will smell out your camper in time. Olive oil is good in Greece en route, but as always, everywhere, expensive. I take equally expensive, poly-unsaturated corn oil from England for the whole trip. You can, however, get corn oil in Pakistan, but not poly-unsaturated.

Soup. Many people like packets of soup which are comforting, but alas, fattening. Chicken Oxo cubes make a good soup, if jazzed up with spices and are a good addition to all forms of meat and vegetable cooking.

Olives, Cheese and Nuts. You can get excellent olives on the way through Greece which will last for a long time if kept submerged in the accompanying brine. We take a number of plastic containers with us for this purpose. The Greek goat's cheese is as good as the olive oil. One can get wonderful cottage cheese in bulk in Turkey and we find it invaluable with olives, tomatoes and bread for a quick midday meal. The hazel nuts of that country are superb. Walnuts, almonds and pistacchio are plentiful in Iran, but not cheap.

Yoghourt. Yoghourt is available, especially from Greece onwards. In Iran it is called 'Mast'. In southern Afghanistan and in Pakistan's North West Frontier Province (NWFP) it goes by the name of 'Mastur' and thereafter 'Dahi'.

Tinned Food. One simply must take some tinned meat and fish. I have found that one tires less of corned beef than any of the more exotic types, but alas, eaten almost unrelieved in long wars and between-war campaigns, it is more than I can now stand even cooked in the many ways we tried in the field. Besides it is very expensive. I am the same about sardines, which are good food. The main thing is to go for variety, although most of the pork and ham products taste much the same. If you have pink, pig-type luncheon meat, it requires loving care in preparation. Warm the tin slightly so that it will slide out intact when opened. Then take a very sharp knife, cut the meat into wafer-thin slices and dump it all in the rubbish bin. There are kinds of tinned food that you can do nothing with.

Tinned Frankfurters are, however, just one example of the occasional change of diet you can achieve. Tinned pig tongues is another. Shop around and see how wide a variety you can include. It will pay off. Highlight your planning with occasional rather more expensive items from the delicatessen department.

I have not yet tried dehydrated meat. Others say it is satisfactory and it is of course far less heavy and bulky than tins. Supermarkets stock it in bulk as well as soya substitute.

Fresh Meat and Eggs. Eggs are excellent, though expensive in Greece. They are fair and not too dear in Turkey and Iran so long as you don't buy them in Teheran where they are supplied from the Shah's farms and could not cost more if gold-plated. In Pakistan, the price is similar to that in England, but quality is only good in Islamabad (the Capital). Meat is good in all these countries and you can get wonderful fish in Turkey.

As I have already suggested, meat is poor in India and in remote places, particularly in the south, not always available. The only thing to do to the meat is to curry it, except in Delhi where you can get good beef and pork. Elsewhere, the meat is mutton so-called, more often goat. The Indian chicken was for a while better bred, but is now going back to skeletal stringiness although you can get good, tiny frozen chickens in Delhi stores. The egg too, pigeon-size when I was first in India, was for a time raised to a better standard, but is now dwindling again and has a pale putty-coloured yolk.

Vegetables and Fruit. Both in India and en route these are generally good and the stalls a delight to the eye. Some of the best fruit in the world grows in Turkey, chiefly in the south rather off the direct route to India. Potatoes and cauliflowers can be got in most parts of India and the former can be used for a marvellous, filling dish – potato curry (see Appendix I) which will cheer up many a dismal tinned meal and can be quickly cooked under pressure. So can cauliflowers. Try Indian vegetables such as brinjals (aubergines), bhindis (lady fingers) and so on. Tinned tomatoes are worth taking since some vitamin C is preserved in them. This applies too to tomato purée. Outside Delhi, tomatoes are poor in India, but can be superb in Turkey.

Curry, Pickles and Spices. I keep harping on curry. Don't be put off by this. It is easy to make and you can regulate the strength to the minutest degree, from a pleasant mild flavour to a real scorcher that will make smoke come out of your ears. My reason for doing so is, as I have indicated, that it improves or conceals dull, musty or poor quality food as well as strong-flavoured meat, like goat.

Get your curry powder and pickles in India or Pakistan. Pickles can be sweet or hot and are what we would call chutney. They are based on mustard oil and to a sophisticated, or shall I say depraved palate, delicious. The hotter and more humid the climate, the hotter and more reviving is the curry. In the more temperate north of the Indian sub-continent food is less hotly spiced. It becomes progressively more fiery through Madras to Ceylon – sorry, Sri Lanka.

We've found the best ready-made curry powder to be Agmark Madras Curry Powder, no. 777 and we get tins in Delhi where we also buy Bedekar's pickles. Purists buy curry spices separately and grind them as they need them, but we do not aspire to this – it's too much like hard work.

Spices for pilaos (*see* Appendix I) are as follows (taken with us being difficult to get in India): Black and white peppercorns, Cinnamon bark, Cloves; (bought in Delhi), Coriander (dhuniya) seeds and leaves, Cumin (zira), Cardamom (lachi) black and white, fresh root Ginger (ardrak), Garlic (lassan), Red pepper (lal mirchi) powdered and whole.

Condiments. Good salt is difficult to get in India, but I won't go into too much detail over condiments which are a very personal choice. Vinegar is poor and if you do any Chinese cooking (ideal for camp life) take your essentials like soya sauce with you on grounds of quality.

Sweets, etc. A supply of sweets, glucose tablets and nibbly things such as Kendal Mint Cake are ideal to help a tired driver and navigator. Something, every half hour or so, keeps one going through the day.

Tea, Milk and Coffee. One needs one battle-winning factor – high octane char (tea) as I have already mentioned. We use a mixture of half Earl Grey (Twining's for preference) and half Indian. We take enough Earl Grey for the whole trip and Indian to see us through the outward journey. On reaching Delhi we buy Darjeeling Flowery Orange

Pekoe from the Lopchu Estate (in a pale blue packet from most stores). The mixture, if stood in a pot for a reverent five minutes and then stirred and poured is to me nectar. Take care not to spoil it with real milk. Disgusting as it is in hygienic western dairies, it is even more revolting in India when you can get it. If not boiled, it probably carries all the diseases of Asia. Boiled milk in tea is one of Britain's permanent legacies to India and a nasty one. Apart from anything else, as Indian cattle are hedgerow nibblers and not grazers, the milk tastes horrid. When the hedgerow diet is varied by strong-flavoured leaves cut off the trees by the herd boys as well as brown paper packaging and rubbish, the milk gets nastier still. We therefore use dried, skimmed milk which being almost tasteless, allows the blessed brew full rein. We take enough for the whole journey with us, but you can get dried milk in Delhi that is not too revolting.

Fresh coffee is very good in India, especially in the south where it is grown. Instant coffee is rather expensive, so take it with you if you like it. Pakistan grows none of her own, so all you can get there is instant, imported and expensive. I will say nothing about the Turkish types one meets en route except that they are just not my kind of coffee.

Alcohol. On your way out the top grade drink in Yugoslavia is Badel Slijovovika (plum brandy) – easy to get in any supermarket in the north. The wines vary. Rubin, obtainable in the south is perhaps the best. The beer is good.

In Greece fair wine is hard to find. The peculiarly Greek retzina can be good, but is strong and its resinous flavour has to be acquired. You can get bad retzina which will dry you out like a kipper. The beer, again, is good.

I can recommend Dikmen red wine in Turkey and it is cheap. There is a good white wine at Ephesus. Locally brewed Tuborg beer is strong and not very much to my taste, nor is the lighter Ephés beer, but they can bring the sparkle back to a rheumy eye after a particularly tedious drive.

You can get Skol beer in Iran which is drinkable and some brands of Vodka are good. Afghanistan has nothing and the NWFP in Pakistan is officially dry. You can get Murree beer in the Punjab and the draught variety is quite good, but of course expensive. Draught beer does not have the preservatives that make drinking bottled beer so deadly.

Beer in India apart from being absurdly expensive is preserved by the addition of glycerine which to me at least is poison – it does something peculiar to one's liver. There is one variety that is less fierce than others, made in Haryana, needless to say by a Sikh company, with a parakeet on the label.

Of the spirits, Solon whisky is just drinkable, but there are some headaches in the bottle. Indian cane rum can be a wholesome drink and is lighter than its Jamaican counterpart. Unlike the latter, it tastes most unpleasant. Soniphil is the best, Hercules fair and so is Rosa. None of these is cheap. Genuine Scotch, etc. is almost prohibitive and often adulterated.

Few of the Indian States have prohibition now, but in the days when I used a primus I once tried to get meths in Madras which was dry at that time. I met enormous difficulties as I threaded my way through the maze of bureaucracy. All the while I was the subject of pitying stares. At last it dawned on me that they thought I was 'on the meth'. Small wonder in a State where on account of prohibition the pursuit of demon alcohol has often led to tragic results. All too frequently whole wedding parties succumb to some alcohol-based concoction provided by a rascally wedding contractor. Varnish has often wiped out whole groups of friends and relations.

Soft Drinks. Kissan orange squash is quite good in India, but expensive and not always obtainable. See if you can squeeze in some from England. Coca Cola is safe since every batch is tested at the parent factory, while fizzies like Fanta and 7-Up are drinkable but again expensive.

Vitamin Tablets. I'm not sure whether these should be food or medicine, but multi-vitamin tablets are essential when fresh food is hard to get or if you are living off a country where quality is poor. They are useful too to dish out to the local population who so often suffer from malnutrition.

QUANTITIES

I think the simplest way to give you some idea to work on with regard to quantities is to tabulate what we take for two people living more off their own resources than off the country on a round trip of six months. This assumes that you take fresh food, already cooked, for the first few days out from home and supplement with fresh food on the journey and in India as you need it.

Flour	..	Wholemeal – 75 lb bag } This assumes one makes most of one's bread White – 21 lbs
Cornflour	..	3 lb (for Chinese cooking)
Biscuits	..	2 cases of 24 pkts each, Plain 4 boxes, Sweet
Butter	..	3 lb
Margarine	..	1 lb
Rice	..	50 lb
Lentils	..	2 x 7 lb bags
Sugar (brown)	..	2 x 7 lb bags
Saccharine	..	20 tablets a day (we use this in tea)
Jam or Marmalade	..	4 x 7 lb tins
Mincemeat	..	2 x 7 lb tins
Marmite	..	6 x 8 oz jars
Cooking Oil	..	5 x 5 litre tins (we use a lot for puris)
Chicken Oxo	..	15 doz tablets (useful in stews)
Soup	..	1 pkt per 4 days (we take none)
Tinned meat and fish	..	1 tin of either a day
Eggs	..	5 doz
Spices	..	1 small drum or jar of each
Salt	..	7 lb
Soya & Chili Sauce	..	2 bottles of each (for Chinese cooking)
Tea	..	Earl Grey $\frac{1}{4}$ lb per week Indian, 1 lb – the rest at rate of $\frac{1}{4}$ lb per week bought locally
Milk	..	2 doz x 8 oz tins dried
Coffee	..	2 tins (we largely drink tea)
Vitamin Tablets	..	1 each per day
Alcohol	..	Bought en route
Orange Squash	..	4 gallons

I do realize that the stores I take myself are pretty lavish. Please don't think I'm a road-snob. It has taken me fifty years or more before I could enjoy this getaway life, and, for the elderly, comfort is the equivalent of survival. At least you may have your youth. Can't you give me some of it?

11. *Domestic Utensils and Equipment*

Cooking and Eating, Hygiene and Cleaning, Bedding, Cigarettes, Firearms, Altimeter, Binoculars, Torches, Cameras, Tape Recorders and Cassettes, Electric Plugs, Sewing Materials, etc., Reading Matter, Radio, Writing Materials, Alarm Clock, Clothes Pegs, Fishing Tackle, Shooting, Painting.

Cooking and Eating. Cooking utensils, cutlery etc. are a matter of personal taste, but don't forget the tin opener, the corkscrew, or for that matter the bottle opener – screw-top bottles are rare. Utensils for making Indian types of bread are best bought in that country. They are very cheap and are listed in Appendix I. You need a very sharp knife or two to deal with that Indian meat, but above all a pressure cooker which I have already mentioned. It saves fuel, time and exasperation as it will reduce the toughest goat into submission. Take spare safety plugs and a spare gasket for the lid. They wear out quickly in India. Be sure you have the recipe book sold with it. Besides this, the following items are almost essential:

A large aluminium kettle
A non-stick frying pan
A large, a medium and a small saucepan. Aluminium/steel are best
    with insulated handles, as small as possible
2 plastic mixing bowls
A selection of plastic containers with lids for storing food

It's no good talking about cooking pots unless one has the means of making fire. Take English matches with you. It's no fun to have a match head down your deep plunge. I suggest the big boxes which are easy to find and less easy to palm.

An aluminium teapot and Insulex mugs, together with plastic plates should do you well. Soda bicarb. will clean the mugs provided one uses it early enough.

I myself like drinking out of gaily painted glasses, but you may have to do without glass if you travel light. Short, wide heavy ones tip over less often than the tall, thin variety. A couple of sets of stainless steel mini-tumblers that fit into each other are useful too.

Thermoses should be big and of good quality. We have three that have knocked about for seven years and are still as good as ever. They are Isovacs with a pouring lip and can be as good for cold drinks as hot. Two of them fit into a flat basket clamped in the cab for a day's run.

Besides your sharp meat knives, keep your tools down to a minimum. You never use very many and they can clutter you up. We have found a palette knife, a flat spoon with holes in for deep frying, a large metal spoon and a couple of wooden ones quite sufficient, together with a small nylon sieve for straining things.

Don't forget to take some cutlery, preferably stainless steel, and make sure the knives are sharp.

Hygiene and Cleaning. A pedal litter bin with plastic liners is invaluable. There are no bounds to what you will use it for in an emergency and the plastic liners make rubbish disposal very simple. The sweeper (Indian cleaner) who empties our bin for us every day in our usual camp loves this system dearly. It is so neat and clean compared with his dirty task of lugging heavy kerosene tins of kitchen refuse to the rubbish dump for crows to fight over.

Klingfilm is useful for covering food, and plastic bags of all sizes are invaluable for all purposes.

A plastic bucket is ideal for your basin drain and is essential for washing the vehicle. I advise a second for washing clothes.

Mafu or Vapona, preferably the former, in small sizes are a 'must' for the fly-blown east. If you expect to spend nights in the hotter parts of the sub-continent, have insect repellent cream for mosquitoes. Netting over the windows makes the camper airless.

You can't have too many cloths – J-cloths, dishcloths, engine grease rags and endless moppers up. One can't carry enough paper tea towels for a long trip, but wash your dishcloths often or get it done for you well and cheaply in eastern countries.

'Sparkle' spray will clean and polish formica surfaces and so does Ajax cream. Washing-up liquid and abrasives are not easy to get in India, but washing powder such as Surf is. Take your own toothpaste, toilet soap, cosmetics and above all razor blades. Toilet paper abroad is generally poor.

Paper handkerchiefs avoid the difficulty of washing and can be got on the way and in India.

Bedding. Sleeping bags are the most popular form of bedding. We find it more hygienic to have them opened flat with easily washed nylon sheets and more comfortable too. Study to be warm. Nights in India and on the way can be cold.

Cigarettes. If you rot your lungs with tobacco, cigarettes are not expensive in Turkey and India, but not always very good. You would be wise to buy your quota on the cross-Channel ferry. Get some anyway, even if you do not smoke yourself. They are useful to pass round among acquaintances on the journey, especially in Turkey. The inhabitants of that country appear to regard it as a kind of divine right to demand them from travellers, so much so that some lorry drivers arm themselves with loose cigarettes to throw out to importunate bystanders on slow and difficult parts of the road in order to avert worse evils. We have never yet found this necessary.

Firearms. Do you carry a firearm? I have thought about this a great deal and have come to the conclusion that it is best not to. First, it is a bore at each border where such weapons have to be declared, since the procedure holds you up. Secondly, it has to be an automatic pistol or a revolver. One can't poke a rifle out of a vehicle window, or a longbow, while an arquebus needs a bit of teeing up. So you are no match for a man in ambush with a rifle or a revolver for that matter, as the initiative is with him and he is behind cover while you are teed up, so to speak, on the fairway. One can't simply go about drawing on somebody who looks as if he might like to shoot you. Think of the piles of corpses. In short, you are more likely to start something that you will not be able to be in at the finish of, if you get me. I did once get out of the middle of a deteriorating riot by waving a .45 about, but that's another tale.

To illustrate the danger – on one trip we saw two young Americans, a donkey and cart and a dog in Turkey walking to India as we were on our way home. We were charmed with the outfit which was trekking on behalf of UNICEF. A year later, on our next trip out we learned from a great friend, Colonel Kush Wakt-Ul-Mulk, descendant of Ghengiz

Khan and uncle of the Mehtar of Chitral and himself a great walker, that the party had met with disaster. He was about to leave Peshawar to meet them at the Pakistan border and walk with them down the Khyber, when he heard that one evening near Sarobi in Afghanistan the young men had seen two armed nomad Pathans robbing and beating up a truck driver. One American foolishly fired his shotgun in the air hoping to scare the robbers off. Whereupon the robbers shot both young men, killing one and severely wounding the other.

Look at it another way: it's better to be robbed than killed and robbed. I have seen one Pathan shoot another in the NWFP and also in tribal territory, in a trivial quarrel over a rupee.

A gun is a valuable object. Indeed in some parts of your journey it is a symbol of manhood. Nomad Afghan and Pathan men feel undressed without one. Therefore your possession of such a weapon may actually provoke attack from thieves rather than avert it.

Altimeter. An altimeter is an interesting and useful device to take. It helps you to choose low altitude camps for the night. After motoring up and down all day you end up with no idea how high up you are. Lauries of Wigmore Street sell a reliable and simple instrument, which you can check en route on the Caspian which is just below sea level.

Binoculars. These are particularly important if you are interested in wild life.

Torches. A map-reading one is essential in case you get benighted. Have also a large one with a red intermittent light in case of night breakdowns, as well as a smaller one. Smaller sized batteries are easy to get in India and good, but the large 6 and 9 volt ones are difficult to find. Torch bulbs are poor and 6 volt ones again difficult.

Cameras. Your own choice of course. It is better to get films developed in England and bring out enough with you. Film is scarce and expensive in India and with the falling value of the pound I doubt if it pays any more to stock up in Europe.

Tape Recorders and Cassettes. Again a matter of choice and they can be run off the mains or your car batteries. If off the batteries, have a suitable convertor with protection against surge to which car batteries are subject.

Electric Plugs. The mains are AC, 220–240 volts, 50 cycle in India and on the way, i.e. just like England, but plugs are triple round pin or two-pin and slightly different in size from English ones. They are easy to get, but lay in a store in Delhi. In countries en route you may have to buy local plugs.

Sewing Materials, etc. Include buttons that may be difficult to match and spare zips.

Reading Matter. Paperbacks in India are much the same price as in England. The choice is not unlimited and largely soft porn. Better books are not very expensive and I have bought some beautiful ones in Delhi on Persian carpets, Mughal miniatures, etc. There are also useful handbooks on Indian wild life to be found.

Radio. You can get world broadcasting services on a short waveband most of the time. This of course requires transistor sets rather than 'car-radios'. Anything with transistors in it must be carefully protected against heat, shock and dust.

Writing Materials. Take some with you, including good biros and refills, as well as notebooks, drawing paper etc. All are expensive, of poor quality and scarce. You can buy air letters in India and Pakistan.

Alarm Clock. This is vital for that early morning start.

Clothes Pegs. Plenty of the plastic kind and a plastic-covered clothes line make the washerwoman's life simpler.

Fishing Tackle. If you are a fisherman, you can get fishing in many unexpected places, but not tackle. There is fly-fishing for trout in Kashmir and Kulu. People usually spin for the fierce Mahseer, fast fading glory of the Indian rivers, but I have had good sport with a fly in small rivers in the winter in the Himalayan foothills.

Shooting. If you like shooting you can take a shotgun and cartridges. Indian cartridges are very poor. Duck, etc. shooting in Kashmir is well organized by the Tourist Bureau. India is largely shot out, but if you make enquiries good shooting can still be found. Remember the delay that taking a shotgun means at borders and that cartridges are heavy.

Painting. If you paint, take your usual kit as it will be difficult to get.

12. *Clothing*

HE

The guiding principle in choosing your clothes should be comfort, combined with ease and speed for you in dressing and in washing them. Do have a bit of style too, for are you not an ambassador? For the winter six months' trip which I do, one needs both very warm clothes and very cool. On the journey in spring or autumn you can be colder than in an English winter and somewhat warmer than in summer. Temperatures largely depend on the height of the country and the influence of the Black and Caspian seas.

Everyone will suit himself, but I favour something easy to pull over the head and shoes to pull on the feet without lacing. Turtle-neck acrilan or other easily washed pullovers are suitable. To these I add long-sleeved cardigans of the same man-made fibres, but of course a different weave. You can have fun with the colours and blend them well. Be cheerful, there's no virtue in drabness. Trousers should be of washable, man-made fibres too (quick drying – no ironing).

Clothing for any specialized activity such as fishing is a matter of taste and your own experience. I do a lot of fishing and wading and find I need a warm, waterproof coat for this and light, rubber-soled canvas shoes. Boots and rubber waders are out of the question as the going is very rough wherever you fish in India and they are too heavy.

You would be wise to take a thin, drip-dry suit, a good shirt and a tie or two as you may get formal hospitality. Indians are very 'correct' in their attire and a business suit is often normal wear for the jungle. A bush shirt and scarf are however quite the thing in the evenings in towns in warm weather.

In the heat certain precautions are necessary, but we of World War II in Burma debunked many of the old shibboleths. We kept fittest in shorts and socks and a beret. Red flannel spine pads, shorts below the knees and cholera belts are nonsense of the past, but of course you know that; though I wouldn't put it past a tropical outfitter to try and flog some to you.

You may like a straw hat. There are all sorts of modern ones with basket-work ventilation and you can take several scarves to go round the crown and match your turn-out. Don't have a leopard-skin band. This brands you as a beginner and a cad. Leopards are to be preserved.

Keep a set of disreputable working clothes including a soft cap for dealing with your engine, etc. You cannot risk getting your better clothes oily on a journey where washing and cleaning facilities may be limited. Even the largest camper has not got room for huge piles of oily garments.

UNISEX

Take sweaters and warm coats such as Huskies. Don't, please, wear duffle coats. They look sloppy with their hoods hanging down and are bulky. The best form of sweater is mohair. The material is expensive, but quick to knit, light, gloriously warm and lasts for ever.

Shoes, apart from being pull-on, should be stout for long walking, if you care for it. Of course, this may be forced on you. Oddly enough for high altitude trekking, tennis shoes with good thick soles are often best, being light. You need quite a few on stony ground. You can get good and cheap Bata jungle boots in India, but they take a long time to put on. Sandals are better without open toes. Indian streets are dusty and open toes scoop up dirt and gravel. Rubber, pull-on 'Choodler' shoes are useful for mud and so are lightweight rubber boots. (Choodler is the trade name for a rubber garden shoe – pull-on – from farmers' stores.)

Take light mackintoshes. You will be surprised how much it rains in India, or at least northern India in the winter. In contrast to this pack your bathing suits, but sunbathe only in sophisticated places such as hotel swimming baths. Otherwise you collect a too appreciative audience.

If you can wear it, nylon is best for underwear since it dries quickly.

Brightly coloured PVC aprons are most useful and protect you from cooking burns and scalds. They can save the engineer's clothes too.

If you wear glasses, have your ordinary prescription tinted – not too dark – for driving. Apart from saving your wrinkles, sunglasses do protect your eyes from insects – I forgot mine once and was half-blind for a week from a collision with a fly while driving.

SHE

It is more comfortable for women to wear trousers, but do have long sweaters and tunics. The east disapproves of glamour pants – be modest in your clothing. Have a few drip-dry summer dresses and one or two long ones which should be very smart as you will be in unequal competition with the sari. If you can't beat them, please don't, don't try and join them. Most European women are too big boned to look anything but ungraceful.

13. *Medical*

Stomach Trouble – Drinking Water, etc., Colds and Worse, Eyes and Ears, Analgesics, Wounds and Bumps, Malaria, Sunburn, Sunstroke and Heat-stroke, Snakebite, Hook Worm, Prickly Heat. OUT-PATIENTS.

Medicines are not expensive in India and are manufactured in the country by firms such as May & Baker, Roche, etc. You cannot always get something as prescribed in this country, but can usually get much the same. Antibiotics do not normally need a prescription. There are doctors and dentists in the large centres though hospitals are pretty ropy. The hospital in the High Commission is allowed only to treat diplomats. There are good chemists in Delhi, but medical facilities outside towns are poor. You will have to rely on yourselves. The remarks below apply to your journey out and back as well.

If there is anything that you have to take regularly, make sure that you have enough with you. Your GP can advise and prescribe for you to cover the obvious situations, though if you are taking medicine out of the country in anticipation of disaster, you, not the National Health, will have to pay for it.

Stomach Trouble – Drinking Water, etc. You should not suffer from this if you eat clean food and don't keep it long. Above all, cover food and standing drinks against flies with Klingfilm or beaded net covers. Some people use the Safari filter for drinking water, but unless you have children with you the ordinary medicated tablets from any chemist are sufficient. Their use is simple, but if you are in an epidemic area, boil your water. Drinking water is usually safe in large towns. Apart from this, be careful about washing up.

If you must drink fresh milk, boil it. Never accept tea with milk in it. You cause no offence if you say you like it without. You never know where the milk's been.

There is an old tradition that vegetables and fruit should be soaked in Potassium permanganate – 'pinki pani'. It is effective only in spoiling them. Clean, running water is far better. Thick-skinned fruit is the safest. Water melons and ground fruit are a trifle suspect, even when washed, as surface water can contaminate them. Melons will give you diarrhoea anyway as you'll eat too many of them, particularly in Turkey where you will see them in tempting piles beside the road to Ankara in October.

Should all precautions prove in vain, some form of sulpha is best for bacillary dysentery. We take some sulphadimidine and you can get sulphaguanidine in India. Amoebic dysentery is just something you must not get – the only cure is an immediate return home.

Going to the other extreme Milpar (unobtainable in India) is useful and can help I am told with the 'almost universal' which bumpy roads encourage.

Colds and Worse. These can be misery for everybody on a journey and you should have a broad spectrum antibiotic with you suitable for chest infections. Indian dust is full of germs so any infection must be regarded warily and treated with antibiotics far sooner than one would do in Europe.

'Cold cures' will alleviate your troubles and I advise a good expectorant cough mixture – again because of the dust. Have throat lozenges for the journey and stock up again in Delhi.

Eyes and Ears. These are again likely to suffer in dusty conditions and I would suggest one or more of the antibiotic preparations – they are not bulky. Warm water and boracic can do wonders for sore eyes.

Analgesics. Have a good supply of these. If you don't need them, others will.

Wounds and Bumps. Stretchy elastoplast with dressings is difficult to get in India. It is usually the waterproof kind that does not stick well. I would advise a packet or two of the strip kind and some broad, elastic adhesive bandage, as well as a crêpe bandage. Sofra tulle is invaluable and so are antibiotic creams, Cicatrin and Burnol. Don't forget some safety pins, and Iodex for sprains, etc.

Malaria. You should not need protection against malaria after September or before mid-May. If you travel through India in the summer heat you must take a prophylactic course continuously until you reach high ground. The authorities are becoming more lax about keeping down the anopheles mosquito. There are cases now occurring even in Delhi and Rajasthan. Benign Tertiary malaria is a wearer-down. Cerebral and others are sudden killers, but more rare.

Sunburn. All the usual advice about sun-tanning slowly applies, but remember you need a powerful sunburn lotion or cream for India, especially if you are high up. You girls will need a darker powder base and powder after a time. Your lipstick will save your lips from chapping in sun or wind, but I hope the men will use colourless lipsalve.

Sunstroke and Heatstroke. Sunstroke is a myth, but avoid glare headaches by using dark glasses. Heat is very definitely a hazard, but not a frequent one. It only strikes those who have poor sweat glands or those who eat and drink alcohol heavily in the heat of the day. It can strike too if you are stretched to the limit, as in warfare in these regions, but I'm not trying to get you a V.C.

If you are much in the heat, take a lot of salt even to the extent of putting it into drinking water. It is a coolant and prevents cramps as well as reviving you. Avoid constipation, and therefore have your favourite aperient with you if you use one.

Snakebite. Europeans seldom get bitten by snakes, though the bare-footed native does. Slacks, socks and shoes are adequate protection. Don't turn over stones with bare hands though; snakes sometimes lie under these. They are at their most prevalent in the monsoon and are also present in the hot weather. Don't think the whole place is crawling – you seldom see them. In the winter they are even less common, so don't picture yourself at your last gasp, wrestling like Laocoon, all wrapped up in serpents. I can never fathom how he and the boys got themselves in such a jam, but of course they weren't wearing anything.

I have only ever met one European who was bitten by a snake. He was a young Swiss wild life photographer who sat up all night in vain over a saucer of milk beside a sacred hole in which there lived a sacred cobra. Came the dawn and he stumbled wearily out of his van, stood on the snake with bare feet and was promptly bitten. Fighting down panic he rushed to the nearest snakebite clinic in Benares for treatment, only to be told repressively that it couldn't have been a very big snake or he'd have died by then – he survived.

Hookworm. Speaking of bare feet, don't go about without shoes. You might pick up hook-worm in the dust and mud near a village. It is difficult to get rid of and unpleasant.

Prickly Heat. This is not dangerous, but is irritating. If you are travelling in the cooler seasons, you should not be bothered by it. Cleanliness and light clothing, preferably cotton, are the best safeguards if you have to travel in the heat. Drink plenty of liquid and use talcum powder sparingly. Babies would suffer if they get it, but if they are of an age where they can't move about much, or are still using nappies, they should not be taken on this kind of journey.

OUT-PATIENTS

As doctors are so few and far between in the country, as a white man you will be expected to help the sick. It is traditional and dates from British times. If you wish to enjoy your holiday, help those who have no other help. It is really worth stocking up with simple medicines in Delhi to this end. Faith in you and no previous experience of antibiotics in your patients will come to your aid, particularly as dosages are always clearly indicated.

The situations that will confront you will ordinarily be much the same as I have mentioned above. I would suggest getting some more analgesics and a really fierce cough mixture for colds. This makes your patients feel they have had something really effective.

People wear poor or no shoes, but still chop about with sharp instruments. Babies frequently roll into open cooking fires on the floor and boils are very common as the result of neglected scratches, scabies and malnutrition. They generally need antibiotic treatment as well as dressings. Epsom salts are excellent for exterior treatment, dissolved in a strong concentration in very hot water. This is useful for getting out thorns and splinters.

Epsoms can be a dynamite aperient in cases of rocklike constipation among your patients. I would advise you to stock up on sulpha for dysentery and something for threadworms, etc. among children, from the Delhi chemists. Make enquiries as to their diet. A small boy was brought to us suffering from violent diarrhoea and no sulpha or anything else did any good until by endless questioning we discovered that his feckless mother stuffed his mouth with brown sugar lumps every time he was tiresome. We stopped the sugar and he recovered at once. This condition is known by the way as 'Dasht' and its opposite 'Kabuz', but I'm not going to teach you all the languages. You are travelling to enjoy yourselves.

There are sure to be cases of Benign Tertiary malaria with its characteristic recurring nature. It is generally one day on and one day off, accompanied by shivering, and your patients will diagnose themselves from experience. It is necessary to sweat out the fever with aspirin before giving the anti-malaria tablets or they may be sicked up. Yellow eyeballs and a hard spleen are other indications. All fever is called 'Bukhar' in India.

This all makes rather dismal reading, but India is not a death trap. The sun counterbalances disease and will be a blessing. You have every chance of returning home fitter than when you left.

Part Two

Part Two

14. *The Backbone – Calais to Istamboul*

Before starting on the route proper, a word about timing and the importance of maintaining the objective.

When one comes to consider the question of time, there are so many imponderables that to calculate a definite number of driving hours per stretch is unrealistic. Vehicles vary greatly in their cruising and top speeds and so do drivers. Traffic conditions vary, particularly in Turkey where one may be held up increasingly between Istamboul and Ankara by the sheer weight of traffic. Bridges can disappear overnight and new roads be unexpectedly opened up. The size of the party greatly affects the speed with which it can get on the road. My suggestions are based on the experience of two people, prepared to get up early in order to complete a stage, by daylight in autumn.

You must, like the good general, maintain the objective, in this case India. To do this I will describe the best and nearly the shortest route – the Backbone. You will be tempted to go down many lateral roads to visit other places on the way, but if you do this much, you will miss the best motoring season on the more rigorous stretches. Later, to whet your appetite, I will take you down some of these laterals, which I will call the Ribs and Limbs. They can become the objectives of other full holidays another year.

Warning: I give you directions to get through the big cities, but you will find that I have interlarded them with asides of one sort or another to relieve the monotony. It is essential therefore, that the navigator reads up the directions before starting, together with the 'through routes' which you have got from the motoring organizations.

THROUGH EUROPE

The quickest way to get through Europe is to follow the motorways from Ostend to Wiener Neustadt. I know this means a detour round the Salzkammergut, but the latter is so beset by fog and the road so bad that it is 'the longest way round'.

On your return when re-entering Germany, don't mention that you have come from India – we did once. At this the official face froze and we were taken out of the vehicle column into a siding. Before the heavily armed interrogator could turn into Hitler, we attacked and Peggy demanded in her best German, 'What is the matter? The Herr General is not in the habit of carrying contraband.' Putting on rank works like magic and the official became very polite. He said he only wanted to see if we were carrying monkeys. Apparently some tourists do try and smuggle monkeys bought in India. Just imagine having monkeys as back seat drivers – dogs are bad enough.

The road from Wiener Neustadt southwards takes you over the Semmering Pass, through Gratz to Yugoslavia which you enter near Maribor. The Semmering is the easiest pass in the late season. Beyond Maribor a new road, not yet shown clearly on the motoring organization routes, takes you down to the motorway (Autoput) west of Zagreb for Belgrade and the south. Some people like to leave the motorway at Niš for Bulgaria. This is the shorter route to Istamboul (the name means 'To the City'), but involves tiresome formalities and poorer roads. Good camp sites are difficult to find and the border crossing near Edirne in Turkey is crowded and bad-tempered. We prefer to continue southwards on the motorway into Greece and travel through Thessalonika and along the coast road to the border at Ipsala, twenty-five miles beyond Alexandropolis. Here your journey really begins.

Via Greece

Calais to the German/Belgian border at Eynatten ..	214 miles
Eynatten to the Austro/German border at Salzburg ..	470 miles
Salzburg via Vienna and Weiner Neustadt to Spielfeld/ St Ilj (Yugoslavia)	360 miles
St Ilj to Gevgeglia (Greek border)	720 miles
Gevgeglia to Ipsala (Turkish border)	286 miles
Ipsala to Istamboul	177 miles
Total ..	2,227 miles

Via Bulgaria

Calais to St Ilj (as above)	..	..	..	..	..	1,044 miles
St Ilj to Niş	..	..	..	..	..	469 miles
Niş to Istamboul via Sofia and Edirne		..	..	..	459 miles

Total   ..   1,972 miles

Estimated time for above: 6 days' reasonable driving

THE TURKISH BORDER TO ISTAMBOUL –
177 miles

It is no good getting there much before eight o'clock in the morning as on the Turkish side they like their zizz. Form filling starts here in the offices on either side.

One year there was a spot of bother – not our bother, but a bit of bother the Greeks had thought up. There was cholera in Istamboul and many Turks, though tough and hardy, have the ignoramus's dread of the needle. Hundreds of them had run away temporarily from the city to avoid inoculation. Greeks never can resist fishing in troubled waters – there is such a long score to settle between the two races. They closed the border for all travellers, including campers leaving Turkey to enter Greece on the homeward run after the summer holiday. This was very awkward for camper parties and Consuls had to come out from Istamboul and feed them and give them money. The Anglo-Saxon doesn't lie down easily in a hold-up like this and the Aussies and New Zealanders doing the run were equally annoyed. When a busload of Greeks who had been holidaying in Turkey blithely drove up to the border expecting to cross back home immediately, the campers started up and made a barrier of their vehicles' much to the Turkish frontier guards' pleasure. One law for all was the cry and the Greeks were turned back. We crossed in the middle of all this and, driving up to the crush of campers early in the morning, tapped on the windows. Flimsy gingham curtains were drawn back and sleepy heads looked out. 'Just take your hand-brake off, old chap and we'll push you back a bit. We'll push you forward again when we're past.'

This we did, rather towering over the mass of combis and the like and got through without much trouble. The Turkish sentries thought it was marvellous.

I always put the family crest on the car, partly because I like showing off and partly because a gold buck impresses officials and sentries who think I must represent an important organization: a nice bit of camper-manship.

There is no super petrol to be got until Istamboul and in October the road is through rather bleak country, unrelieved by summer wheat. The surface is fair and the road straight, with steep climbs and dips. What a difference from a few years ago when it was all varying degrees of corrugated scrape. In those days one was already a bit punch drunk after a few early battering rounds in Yugoslavia and the worst part of the journey was still to come. Watch out for cross winds here – at times one fights with the wheel to counter the next gust.

You join the coastline of the Sea of Marmora at Tekirdag and from there run along beside the shore towards Istamboul, joining the road from Bulgaria some thirty-five miles farther on. Traffic thickens now, but it is not really heavy. The worst difficulty is the downhill Charlies. The road is still steeply up and down and one is bullied by its kings, driving fast Benz buses. At heart the Turk is still a nomad on a horse and expects his vehicle to jump an obstacle at the last moment. The bus driver has great prestige in a poor land and he shows no mercy. He will cut in at a hair's breadth, but flash him up with your lights and sound your doomcracker horn and he will show you some consideration, though he has the legs of us all.

Camps at Istamboul. Seven miles short of the city, on the dual carriage-way just after the turning to the airport you will see the bright flags of all nations at the BP Mocamp and service station of Kartal Tepe, on the right. This is a good halting place for servicing and a breather. It is well appointed from the angle of WCs, ablution, laundry and parking. Turks are very cleanly in spite of lack of facilities in the villages. The bar and meal service has become very off-hand and casual of late. It used to be good. I blame the taggle-haired, taggle-bearded tourist for this. General scruffiness breeds contempt, for many loiter here rather aimlessly and some founder. However, oil change and routine servicing are still quickly and efficiently done at little more than the cost of the oil.

It so happened that last time we came through, we went to the Shell service station half a mile farther on as the BP was being rebuilt. There are other camps and halting places near the coast and beyond the city on the Black Sea, but these two above are the most convenient.

The Shell station was just finishing its ablution and cooking areas and is probably overall the better bet as it has an easier entry and more room. There are two parking areas – one as usual among gardens with hard standing for campers and the other an enormous paved area for lorries. There the mammoths of the road stop in large numbers before attempting the mountains. It is like a busy seaport and there is something of the same atmosphere. Mix and talk with the drivers of the transporters. They have a difficult task and are men of great character and a sense of adventure. They will help Joe Mutt if he's got tangled up with the electrics again. They roll in and park in lines with remarkable dexterity. You may have parked the night before in a specially selected open space, to wake up next morning to find a wall of monsters all round, quite close, though generally they will have left your exit clear. With their sixteen gears and big, expensive diesels which tick like clocks they will not have woken you up. I always feel that these great argonauts look down kindly on our three-and-a-half-ton midget like solicitous female elephants.

As your thoughts dwell on the journey eastwards from Istamboul you will remember, if you've been before, the steep passes ahead, day after day till you get to the great Tahir Pass and beyond that the even more exposed Irek Gecidi (pass) with the Haraz and the Bojnourd later on in Iran. What are we all worrying about? The Asian Highway is completed now and it shouldn't be too tough for a good camper, though one ought to get through before the threat of snow as October draws on.

It is, however, a narrow, steep horse-shoeing journey for the container traffic. There are now so many of them that the roads, especially in poorer Turkey, cannot keep up. During the heavy snow and bitter cold of winter it is impossible to keep repairs going, so that stretches are reverting almost to the condition of twelve years ago. Many of the steep climbs are across narrow causeways of unstable shale, and being narrow the road cannot wind in horseshoes. It goes straight up the slope surprisingly steeply and the bumpy surface snubs off one's planned acceleration to rush it. It is not surprising that the container drivers get nervous, for they cannot choose the season to cross, though at times in mid-winter the road is impassable. Collected at the Shell station, they tell each other stories while the morale drops and drops. It is not uncommon for a driver to lose his nerve, leave his vehicle and fly home. In fact the 10.30 a.m. plane out of Istamboul is known as the Drivers' Special.

The City. Depending on what time you arrive at the service stations, you have to decide whether to stop there or carry on across the Bosphorous to Asia. It is of course a good stopping place for seeing the sights of the city itself, if you are not bonnet down for the east. There is so much to see, so much history, so many names – the Second Roman Empire that lasted nearly a thousand years, the Crusades, the Ottoman Turks, the Sick Man of Europe, the Lady with the Lamp, Ataturk dying in the Dolmabace – one could go on for ever conjuring up the past. I can only suggest the atmosphere of the place. For more, you must go and see for yourselves and consult a guide book. I must confess that to stand under the dome of Aya Sophia, sad and gloomy though it now is, was the fulfilment of a childhood dream. A lot of the guide books seem to forget the mosque of Suleiman which is to my mind far finer than the Blue Mosque and so many people never hear of the Kariyē, small and forgotten near the city walls whose severe frescoes and brilliant mosaics form such a splendid memorial to the Comneni dynasty. You could spend days in the Topkapi Palace with its collection of celadon and blue and white china, whose stone pavilions and buildings look like tents of an untidy encampment and house collections of splendid pictures and jewels like boiled sweets.

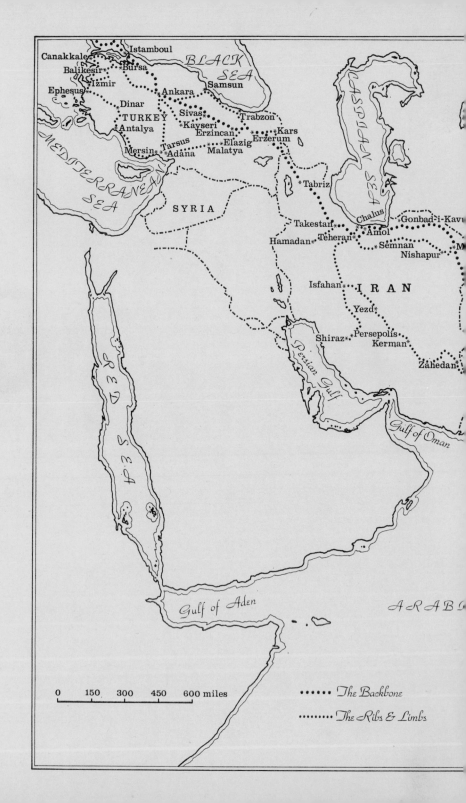

The Backbone
The Ribs & Limbs

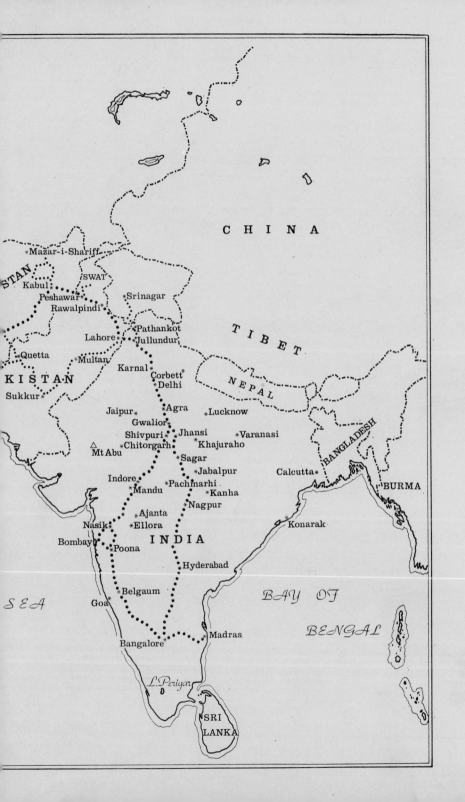

15. *The Backbone – Istamboul to Ankara*

DISTANCES AND TIMES

Istamboul to Ankara .. .. 280 miles 1 day

Through the City. An early start from Istamboul will get you to Ankara by the evening. The roads are well signed throughout Turkey, in Roman script, and distances indicated every ten kilometres. There is super petrol at most BP and Shell stations as far as Ankara and thereafter at Yozgat, Sivas and Erzerum.

From the camps carry on down the dual carriageway up to the old walls of Istamboul, or perhaps Byzantium would be more appropriate as they were built long before the Ottoman Turks swept in from Central Asia. Enter the city by the Topkapi Gate, now only a hole in the walls which have been torn down at this point to make room for the sacred combustion engine and continue straight ahead over the fly-over by the Ak Saray Mosque on the left, up the hill, then past the Bayazit Mosque, again on the left close to the covered bazaar, past the University and the Cemberlitas (Constantine's Column) and down the hill to the enormous square in front of Aya Sophia. To recognize it, look for a buff-coloured dome with grilles, a huddle of younger domes and minarets, tall, slim, spiky towers like chimneys. Over to your right lie the Hippodrome and the Blue Mosque.

Here, turn sharp left and follow the trolley buses down a narrow, cobbled, dark and dingy street to the wide open area in front of the railway station. Now turn right, getting into the left-hand stream of traffic, as you will turn left at the bottom of the square. Once round this corner, edge back into the right-hand stream, ready to cross the Galata Bridge over the Golden Horn. By now you have had your first taste of the Istamboul traffic, but there isn't much to worry about. The more timorous can leave the camps at 6 a.m. to avoid the rush when the whole world seems madly bent on getting to the centre of the city, on foot or in huge American taxis that stop in front of you without warning to pick up fares. For some reason the black and white chequered band painted round their waistline makes them look like sharks, sharks that are best avoided. Remember to keep the initiative, be quick on your gears and bully your way through with the other bullies. Use the outer lane a good deal on the dual carriageway if you are right-hand drive, since it protects your left flank. Remember too that all pedestrians are jay walkers and veiled women wet hens, so keep your eyes very wide open.

On this journey you'll soon become superstitious and do all sorts of things to ward off the evil eye and ear. Never say, 'When we get to such and such a place, we will do so and so,' without an elaborate ritual of touching wood and everything else you know. If you don't, ten to one you'll not get there that day.

To return to the Galata Bridge: at the other end bear right along the quay with the one-way stream of traffic and follow this stream until you reach the T-junction with the Necati Bey Street where you turn right again along the coast.

The One-way Traffic on your Return. On your way home follow the one-way traffic from this point in the opposite direction, looking for the signs for Avrupa (Europe), which will take you over the Galata Bridge, back to Europe. You have to turn right as you leave the foot of the bridge, but edge into the left-hand stream and turn left round a hairpin almost immediately. Edge right here and turn up right, into the square in front of the railway station. You go straight up the side of the square and straight on up a narrow street, half left and up again over the cobbled shoulder of a hill (Istamboul is all built on hills). This brings you to a T-junction with your original road by the University and the Cemberlitas.

Crossing the Bosphorus – The Bridge. You drive along Necati Bey Street on the coast past the Dolmabace Palace, a large, grey, ornate building on the right pretending to be Versailles, and go straight ahead until you see the sign for the new suspension bridge across the Bosphorus – the sign is just the picture of a bridge. Turn right and cross the road by a fly-over and then up a long hill as far as the sign for Ankara. Turn right on to the motorway which takes you over the bridge and on again to join the main route to the capital. The charge at the toll gate is 50 lirasi for two people and a big camper – about the same as the ferry. On your return, take the first road leading off the motorway after crossing the bridge in order to reach the coast road again. If you stay on the motorway you will end up lost in the middle of Galata, possibly never to be seen again.

The Ferries. Before the bridge was built we used to cross by the ferries and you can still do it if you prefer it. They are very efficient but not as quick as the bridge. One often had to queue for some time as the traffic used to be very heavy. The queues form just short of the Dolmabace and are controlled by the police, well and firmly. One takes one's ticket before boarding the boat which is a drive-on and drive-off one. While you are waiting, buy rings of bread and sesame seeds from a vendor. They are delicious. The ferries take you to Usküdar (Scutari) and as you drive off you bear right up the hill following the general stream of traffic, past an old Turkish cemetery until you see a rather small sign for Ankara where you turn right and soon join the motorway. In the distance you can see the hospital where Florence Nightingale revolutionized military nursing.

Usküdar to Bolu Dagi – 146 miles. The route to Ankara is dual carriage-way for the first thirty miles or so through villages where it is easier to shop for bread and other food than in Istamboul where parking is a problem. Only summer visitors will taste Smyrna figs and the peaches of Bursa, but autumnal fruit is excellent including apples, grapes and bananas. The Turks are not receptive to sign language, but the shop-keepers are pleasant and do not generally cheat one. One great advantage is that they use the same figures as we do and can write down the prices. In any case your shopping will be supervised by friendly passers-by, wishing to help the stupid and pleasantly mad foreigner. If you don't understand the coins, put some out on the palm of your hand and the shopkeeper will pick out the ones he wants, closely watched by your new guardians. A few words of Turkish, as in every country, work wonders. Turks seldom speak other languages, but often claim to speak French. They don't really know it when you switch to it. 'Good Morn-ing', is Merhaba and 'Good-Bye' is Gulë, Gulë. With these two words you are half-way to international entente. Yok for 'No' and Evet for

'Yes' give you a great command of the tongue. For other expressions see Appendix II.

The road takes you through Izmit, the naval port, along the Esplanade and there you leave the Sea of Marmora. The most interesting place you next pass is Lake Sapança with its lovely placid waters. There are a few rather small parking places by the lake, but we generally have other ideas. After seventy-five miles the road starts rising and in ten miles you reach the top of the Bolu Dagi (Pass), at 3,280 ft. It is very steep in places and gives one a foretaste of the gradients to come after Ankara. There is a good service area with restaurants, a motel and a wonderful view half way up and another just completed near the top. The former is delightful and if the weather is kind one can drink a bottle of Dikmen in the sun at an outside table and have a superb meal cheaply. If you left Istamboul early in the morning you will be there about lunchtime. It fits in well as a night stage on the return journey and I am always ready to drive on in the dark to get there, if I'm behindhand or have overstretched. There is generally a watchman who will keep an eye on the vehicle for a small sum. It always pays to have one's own robber in charge so that one will not be tampered with.

Bolu Dagi to Ankara – 134 miles. From now on there is an increasing prospect of good weather in October. I have known rain almost non-stop from home to Izmit and I fear once as far as Mashhad early in the month. It's a toss-up, but at least you are forestalling dangerous snow which one should not trifle with. Take comfort as you will soon get all the glorious sun you want – I suppose one will start complaining of the heat before long.

The run down from the top of the Bolu is far less steep on the Ankara side since you are now beginning to stay up on an average at 2,000 ft. The road is fair and very up and down. It is winding too and one can be very badly held up by slow, heavy traffic of which there seems to be an increasing amount each year. One has to be patient for one will get there some day.

The highest pass is the Civcan Dagi at 4,920 ft. The area is clothed in conifers – a great delight as one does not see trees so much from now on. The scenery is magnificent and on the return journey in spring the hillsides are a mat of crocuses, both yellow and mauve. In Turkey one sees flowers growing wild which one would treasure in one's rock garden.

Great gardens such as Kew send parties to look for new flowers and bulbs and have recently discovered several new varieties of crocus in Eastern Anatolia. There is very fine trout fishing in the summer and some shooting.

One of my earlier diesel campers gave a gasp and fainted on this pass. I was even worse with engines then than I am now and was glad when a smart Turkish road patrol pulled up almost immediately. They are part police and part recovery supervisors. They wear automatics at all times. The two patrolmen were very handsome with the crisp black wavy hair which is a feature of the Turk and close-clipped moustaches. They took off their tunics and worked with a will. I think they were nearly as mystified as I was at first, but after a great deal of undoing and doing up got the engine started. They handed me a part for which they could not find a place – a rather important supporting bolt, and sheared another on the cover of the funny-looking box you open to bleed the air out of the fuel system. But they tried very hard and I was grateful. One got oil on his pullover, but refused the offer of another out of my stores. They even refused, in a non-selfrighteous way, the offer of a cup of tea explaining that as it was Ramadan they couldn't accept it. They were a nice couple of men who had not seen my particular engine before. The point is they got me to Ankara where I got help.

Ankara. As you close on the city, look for the BP Mocamp on the right at Süzuzkoy, thirteen miles out. This is the best place to stop if you want to do any sightseeing. The parking is sufficiently far back from the road to minimize the noise of the traffic.

Ankara is by no means a sightseer's dream and the climate is vile. Curious that Constantine and Ataturk should both have selected sites for their new capitals with really unpleasant climates. Byzantium had and still has a hot, steamy summer and a bitter winter with snow and cruel winds sweeping in from the Black Sea. Ankara is not only bakingly hot and dry in the summer and cold in the winter, but being in a depression like a saucer suffers from a cloud of smog from fires and factories all through the winter. It hangs over the city like a black pall. We spent a pleasant few days there with the then Military Attaché, an old friend, on our first journey, but we were spoilt. There are the remains of Roman baths and temples as well as a very fine Hittite museum. Alexander pivoted on Ankara before he turned south again towards the Cilician

Gates, but there is no trace of his passage. We often find ourselves following his track on this journey and on others when we have been down in the south of Turkey and Iran, even to crossing the Dardanelles where he crossed with his forces at the beginning of his great campaigns.

The Ataturk Mausoleum, though modern, is neither brash nor vulgar. Some of the work, notably the inlaid ceiling, has been done by Iranian craftsmen. Around the huge courtyard there are small buildings containing the relics of this great and colourful man. His car is there, no longer to be guided by his strong hand, that guided the fortunes of his country out of a slough. All I can say is that it is solemn and large and I liked the long avenue with neo-Hittite lions and the typical colourful hills of Turkey in the background. Wear your better clothes if you visit it – the Turks would be put out if you turned up disrespectfully in jeans.

Through Ankara. When you leave the BP station to continue your journey, carry on along the dual carriageway into which the road soon develops. Pass the military airfield on the right and some way farther on go under a big fly-over. The road then swings right and you come up to a crossroads with traffic lights. Edge into the left-hand stream of traffic and turn left here in the direction of Samsun and Corum. There are small workshops and spare part dealers in the small streets to the left after this turning. From here you continue straight on in a wide right-hand curve round the city and up a steep hill lined by military barracks. There is a crossroads at the beginning of the hill and traffic lights. The road to the left goes to the Airport and that to the right to the business quarter where you will find the various motor agents and plenty of spares. At the top of the hill you swing right, still making for Samsun and Corum and set off down the 2 (E23) route.

16. The Backbone –
Ankara to the Iranian Border

DISTANCES AND TIMES					
Ankara to Sivas	..	..	..	278 miles	1 day
Sivas to Erzinçan	..	..	..	156 miles	} 1 day
Erzinçan to Erzerum	..	..	..	120 miles	
Erzerum to Bazargan	..	..	..	200 miles	

From Erzerum you should be able to cross the border at Bazargan and get to Maku 15 miles beyond in 1 day.

Total, Ankara to Border 754 miles.

ANKARA TO SIVAS – 278 miles

All too soon after leaving the capital you start climbing and from there on will be on the toughest part of the journey. There are several petrol stations suitable for night stops here just outside the city. The road surface varies, but it is in general fair in spite of the inevitable frost damage.

Shortly after Cerikli, about eighty miles out of Ankara the road divides. Bear right towards Yuzgat and Sivas. You are still on the 2 (E23). The other prong of the road leads straight ahead towards the Black Sea and Samsun, a longer, tougher route which I will describe later in Chapter 25. On the Sivas road you are, however, seldom below 4,000 ft and often higher. All should be well if your camper is well. This stretch is the most exhilarating motoring. It is here that one really drives making full use of the gears, but not over-revving in any of them. You wind up several hundred feet only to lose the advantage in a long, brake-nursing descent, equally steep, and then up again. It is like motoring along the edge of a saw and the remarkable thing is that one is really motoring along the grain of the country. Motoring from north to south is across the grain in Turkey and is quite a grind. I always nurse my engine a bit, throttling back just off full speed on the hills in each gear and nowadays watching a rev counter. There is an art in changing up and getting up to full speed at the end of a down run which has been carried out in low gear most of the way to save the brakes. With this last minute spurt your impetus will carry you a surprisingly long way up the next mountain side. Be careful though, not to overrun your engine like a downhill Charlie. His vehicle does not belong to him. Change down early rather than late and you may hold the next gear longer, but change that if need be for a lower gear in good time. A four-speed gearbox is quite adequate – do not let me mislead you – but five gears are better and more fun. Remember, your engine is *not* howling because it's in pain or out of breath – it is happy and singing, so do not spare your ears, spare the car.

How the almost legendary English 'Milord' in his Silver Ghost would have loved this drive as a greater alternative to the Alps. Now, that is to say, that the roads are relatively smooth compared with the awful tracks of a very few years ago. He would have had the quality and reliability, but probably not the steam or brakes.

There are not many road patrols after Ankara, but there are powerful little Chevrolet pick-ups that will help you. They usually belong to the Highways Department or to the Post and Telegraphs. Freight drivers will nearly always stop if you are in a difficulty for there is a great brotherhood on these roads. Most campers are midgets here and no problem to tow if need be. What about that nylon towing strap now? If the sun is shining and your engine sweet, it may still only be a case of driving over to India for the winter, old boy and absolutely nothing to it.

Sivas – Camp. Four miles short of Sivas there is a fly-over on to the by-pass to Erzinçan and Erzerum. Currently it is a scrape road, but should be taken because Sivas is crowded and the streets on the farther side of the town narrow and cobbled. Children throw stones at any vehicle. In Sivas Ataturk proclaimed the foundation of the new Turkish state. Its other claim to fame is that it was a garrison town in Roman times.

If you want to stop the night, and it makes a good stage out of Ankara, carry on straight ahead under the by-pass to the small BP camping site, half a kilometre on the left. Get the key for the inside W.C. from the petrol pump attendant as the outside one is horrific. Incidentally, just before you get to the fly-over there is a group of shops on the right-hand side of the road. You can get fruit, eggs, bread and groceries and the shopkeepers are extremely pleasant.

SIVAS TO ERZINÇAN – 156 miles

Retrace your way next day as far as the fly-over and make the wide detour round Sivas. It is a straightforward up-and-down road as before. When you get to Zara, forty-five miles on, fill up with petrol again, although it is not premium. Petrol can be scarce on the next stages of the journey and the quality is suspect at Erzinçan.

At Zara, turn right in the direction of Imranli, Rifahiye and Erzinçan. This is a new road with good tarmac the whole way which cuts out the roundabout, high and stiff route through Serefiye and Suşehri, through which one was formerly directed. There is a long, but not unduly high pass between Zara and Imranli, twenty-three miles away. Nineteen miles beyond Imranli you toil up to the top of the Kizilrakimdag (7,020 ft). This is not a difficult pass for Turkey, and far less steep or long than the Karabeyir Gecidi (6,316 ft) on the other route from Zara. Although that is lower, it has some hair-raising horseshoes on the descent on the eastern side – I would not care to try it on the way home, and never have. There are snowploughs at the top of the Kizilrakim – a snow-plough can take you over in snowy conditions if you stick, but for God's sake tell them to go 'yawash, yawash' – slowly, slowly.

The valley to Rifahiye on the other side of the pass is narrow in places and can be very cold in spring with frost and snow late in the season. It is about twenty-five miles long. The long slow climb to the Sakultutan Pass (6,890 ft) begins after Rifahiye and lasts twenty-three miles. It is not difficult from the west, but on the return journey is quite an obstacle as it is two thousand feet above Erzinçan, twenty-five miles away. Go straight through the town along the high street, towards Erzerum.

ERZINÇAN TO ERZERUM – 120 miles

The road is now tarmac all the way. Until quite recently one used to leave Erzinçan in a cloud of dust and bump round the base of the hills until one reached the Kara Su (Black Water) Gorge, but now there is a direct and splendid road. You drive along beside the river as far as

Terçan, some seventy miles on, at first through a spectacular gorge and later across wide, sunny plains. Just before you get there, there is a marked camp site, on the left. The residents are road menders and, if at home, will make you welcome. They are nice old men and keep bees. There is an inside W.C. and water.

You then cross a low pass and drop down to Askale, thirty-five miles short of Erzerum. This is a point on the journey where one should study the weather. If it is cold, you might be wiser to stop at Askale; just beyond the town there are good and sheltered pull-offs where we have camped wild several times: that is if you have not decided to stay with the beekeepers. Askale is at 5,300 ft and Erzerum, a military head-quarters, a thousand feet higher, open to all the winds. The country beyond is equally high and still colder. The BP site on the Asian High-way is exposed. The last time we stopped here we found the site closed as a result of hooliganism. There are hotels, but they are a bit basic, generally crowded and in any case not for travellers such as we. The Seljuk mosques are worth seeing, but on the whole it is a dreary, cold garrison town. Avoid mechanics there like the plague as they charge the earth and if they cure one ill will create others. There are many shops with a wide range of spares and tyres and if you have trouble, try and repair it yourself or do it at a petrol station where someone will drive up and offer help.

If one lies back at the warmer Askale area, one should easily carry the somewhat formidable Tahir Pass beyond Erzerum and get down well beyond by daylight the next day. The main road skirts the town of Erzerum and you should follow the signs for Iran Huddudu (border) up the hill the other side.

ERZERUM TO BAZARGAN – The Border
200 miles

Remember there is no more premium petrol after Erzerum until Marand, a hundred and twenty-five miles inside the Iranian border. Fifty-two miles from Erzerum is the small town of Horasan. Here the tarmac ends and you turn off on a scrape road to the right on the route signed Iran. A couple of kilometres before you get to the town there is a large petrol station on the left that makes a good halting place if the weather is propitious, especially on the return journey. Many of the juggernauts stop here, and there is a small charge of about 50p. levied by the owner, and a grim W.C.

The top of the Tahir Pass is twenty-two miles farther on and you climb from 5,052 ft to 8,122 ft – no joke on a narrow and bumpy scrape road with tight hairpins. However, the climb should be well within the power of any healthy engine, if not absurdly overloaded. In late October, you should not be held up by snow. We have been backwards and forwards at that time, and in late March and late February some sixteen times and only once have we been slightly checked due to snow, though we have driven through light falls. That time a truck had slid off the road the night before and had to be hauled back across it by a snowplough. We were held up about half an hour. This was in late October and the snow at the sides of the road was not too deep. I have returned twice in late February and got over on packed ice without mishap, though it was somewhat frightening. But stick to late October and early April for this difficult area. In early October you run up against rain and mud – Turkish mud sticks like concrete to your underside and has to be hosed off thousands of miles later with power sprays. One can avoid the pass by going straight on from Horasan to Kars, near the Russian frontier and from Kars direct to Dogubayazit, twenty-two miles short of the border. This route is eighty miles longer than the first, but has no passes of any note. The road from Horasan to Kars is good, but the next stretch is very bad indeed and officially not recommended for heavy traffic – light cars only.

The Tahir is a double pass with a deep fall and a village in between, so go easy on the cheers when you are over the first at 8,122 ft as the next is nearly as high at 7,844 ft. The first big climb finishes up some magnificent horseshoes and you have a wonderful view from the top over the mountain ranges. Watch out for stone-throwing and demands for cigarettes in the village.

You drop to Eleskirt, twelve miles farther on at the bottom of the pass. After negotiating its narrow, cobbled streets, keeping a sharp look-out for stone-throwers, you come to tarmac of a sort again. In this dreary little town a schoolboy stooped to pick up a whole cobblestone, but doomcracker rang out and he nearly fell on his nose. School children in Turkey are generally well turned out in uniform and sometimes wear military peaked caps, even the girls. They march about a lot, but when they are loose they make up for it and are an absolute pest. Stones and indecent exposure are their greeting to visitors. Why can't the eastern parent instil a little discipline in the home? Wave to the little beasts in a sycophantic effort to beguile them from stone throwing. So far, we have only been dented a little in the rear as our devastating horn and minatory pointing at the would-be stone-throwers has saved our windscreen. But one must watch all the time for that child, often a girl, who suddenly stoops, and then one must sound off. Child behaviour in this area is only equalled in Afghanistan and the Khyber.

Looking back over what I have written I feel that it has all been about the difficulties of the route through Turkey. The struggle has its reward in the wonderful scenery the whole way, from the lion-coloured hills round Ankara to the rocks farther east – green, red, ochre and purple. All the colour is so brilliant and the skies deep, deep blue as one climbs up into the eastern plateau. The scarcity of trees makes the slender poplars beside the streams doubly precious – golden poplars and silver willows in the autumn. The women wear brilliantly coloured clothes, colours such as one does not see again until southern India, as they work in the stubble fields or trudge ahead of their husbands, riding on the family donkey.

From Eleskirt onwards the road is awful as it is narrow and damaged by frost. One goes through one medium-sized town full of soldiers, with hideously cobbled streets and the largest potholes I have ever seen. This is Agri, and thirty-eight miles farther on one comes to the Irek Gecidi (6,570 ft) which I have mentioned before. This is no problem on the outward journey in October, but can be very tiresome on the homeward run. Even well on into April there can be snow showers there and often deep mud at critical places.

After Dogubayazit you pass Mount Ararat on your left. This completely symmetrical cone, rising straight out of the six thousand foot plateau to a height of 17,000 ft really is the mountain famous in mythology and in most religions. We once caught it totally unveiled by cloud and could admire the silver sides of the even more cone-like, smaller attendant, which we call Aramouse. I remember once camping at the foot of these two mountains on a clear, moonlit night on our way home in the middle of February. I'm not a botanist, but the weed poking through the snow had a strong, sweet scent. I think it was artemisia. It was astringently cold so that the mind was numbed, too numb really to feel the full icy beauty of the scene. The two mountains glittered like silver and a wolf howled far away.

The Border. There is an element of strategy in crossing the border at Bazargan with its difficult approaches from the Turkish side. If you have started from Askale, you should be able to get over the border before it closes and darkness falls, but may get no farther than Maku on the other side. Remember you are driving against the sun so that to the early darkness of this time of year is added the time change. The clock jumps on a good hour as you enter Iran and the border usually closes at sunset. It opens rather late in the morning, at half-past eight. It is possible to stop short of the frontier at the so-called Tourist Motel in Dogubayazit, but it looks bleak and noisy and we have always managed to get across.

The approach to the frontier post is narrow and the courtyard through which the road goes is very small. The parking and manoeuvring is tedious in a very tight space, but self-appointed traffic directors do give you preference as tourists over the heavy freighters in return naturally for financial recognition. Ten lirasi are ample but make sure they get to the right person. There will be a third person hovering ready to pounce like an Arctic Skua the minute your hand comes out of the window and make off with the tip he has not earned. You have to get out of your vehicle here and go into the offices on the right of the courtyard. I would advise you to wear boots – it is always muddy. Formalities are brief and quick and soon, if the crowd is not too great, you can extricate your vehicle and set off again.

17. The Backbone – The Iranian Border to Teheran

DISTANCES AND TIMES

Bazargan to Tabriz	..	..	..	..	175 miles
Tabriz to Takestan	..	..	..	..	268 miles
Takestan to Teheran	..	..	..	..	130 miles

$\left.\begin{array}{l} \\ \\ \end{array}\right\}$ 1 day

130 miles 4–5 hours

(Traffic is very heavy after 6 a.m.)
Total, Border to Teheran 573 miles

The Border. Having finished with Turkey, inch your way through a not very wide gateway into the Iranian side, another courtyard full of vehicles – many of them broken down and abandoned. The process is long and tedious. Passports are taken away from you and then put in front of you to fill in forms giving the details already in your documents. These are in duplicate, but fortunately there is a carbon. Your forms are laboriously translated into Arabic script in a large ledger. Everything has to be stamped by a senior official who keeps disappearing from his office. When you get your passport back, there will be a pink slip in it – the undersheet of your details. Guard this with your life as far as your exit border. If you lose it, you will be in endless trouble. I have seen this happen. Car documentation and Customs are as described in Chapter 4, and when formalities are complete the official will insist on looking inside the vehicle, clutching your passports and papers to him in case you should suddenly try to drive away. You wouldn't get very far through the solid mass of vehicles jamming the exit. We usually get only a perfunctory glance because he is interested in the type of vehicle and is charmed by my flowery Persian – the formula goes, 'Will the honoured Sir deign to inspect my humble abode?'

Being assured you have no guns or drugs the official returns the documents together with a gate pass. Among the documents is a form that must be produced as you leave the country, so put that with your pink slips.

You still have to add an insurance certificate to the gate pass. The word in Persian is Bime, pronounced beemay. Call this out in a questioning way and you will be directed to that place where the office has settled for the day. Last time the manager had a streaming cold and insisted on giving us a cup of tea. The purser was sacrificed for this and was gloomily certain for the rest of the day that she would sicken and die.

If one survives, the double crossing takes from one to two hours. It is not so terrible for sensible people, but I, being a thruster, find it hard to keep my cool. I do keep it, but I feel like a corked-up reactor – the pressure is awful.

Signposting and Road Patrols. Roads in Iran are adequately signposted at two kilometre distances with figures in Arabic and western numerals. Names are generally in Roman script.

There are traffic police stationed at the fairly frequent weighbridges in smart blue and white cars. They are not very active on the roads. The one time we really needed help in a blizzard on an icy road, the patrol car swept past, blue lights flashing and fat, ringed hands waving benevolently as I held up my red triangle. A big Samaritan cotton lorry answered the signal as we were resigning ourselves to a freezing death and towed us to our haven four miles away on a nylon strap, really bringing home the advantages of this method of towing.

Point duty police in towns are very obliging and helpful, but very firm about directing one down routes for lorries only, if one is large.

BAZARGAN TO TABRIZ – 175 miles

Maku. At Maku, fifteen miles away from the border you go down a steep hill through a town that has trebled its size in the last ten years. I remember it as a village when we first saw it, but now there are some good mechanics' shops as well as everything else that one can need. The bread here is very good and the bakery is on the left in the middle of a row of shops just after the entrance to the Inn. A small sign high up on the right points to this hostelry. It is a pleasant small area with a rough and ready restaurant nearby which serves Skol beer and an eatable meal. It is the one inn I know in Iran where they will let you sleep in your camper for a small parking fee.

There is cheap normal petrol just after you cross the border and again at Maku, as you leave the town, on the right. Refrain from trying to bathe in it in your joy at its cheapness. Iranian petrol stations are marked by a red and black triangle on the site and are thirty to fifty miles apart. The distance to the next petrol station is usually signed in from about ten kilometres distance on this stretch of the journey.

Khoy – the Buzorg Restaurant. If you have the daylight and are still fresh, I would advise you to push on to the Buzorg Restaurant, just beyond the main turning right to Khoy, about seventy-five miles from Maku. Keep straight on the main road past this turning and you will soon see the restaurant and filling station outlined in lovely coloured lights, if you have been driving in the dark. It is a most welcome sight after a hard day.

I don't know why I like the restaurant so much as a stopping-place. Perhaps it has the charm of an oasis in a desert, for it stands in a salty waste. It is pleasant inside and a few locals from Khoy drop in wearing hippie dress to look at the telly and quiz the European girl travellers. Last time most of the travellers were solid Bulgarian and German truck drivers, so their trouble was wasted. But not quite as there was a party of young English people over in one corner, all of them gay and cheerful. We went over to talk to them and found that they were a group of teachers on their way to Australia in a Bedford camper. After the usual pleasantries we also found that they came from the next town to ours and bought their camper through the same agent. Lots of talk about small worlds. They were delightful, full of enterprise and enjoying every minute of their journey. They had had alternator trouble at Belgrade, but had managed to buy and fit a Bosch dynamo instead, which worked fairly well. We met them again later on in India, still cheerful and still making their way to Australia.

We all ordered Skol and a simple meal to follow when we had relaxed a bit. One has to be quite firm almost everywhere in the world to prevent a meal being dumped in front of one before one has assuaged one's thirst, uncoiled and gained an appetite.

The restaurant is a strange little set-up, but very well placed for the traveller. Don't fill your water cans here. The water is very brackish, as is the fishless river. You can fill with water at any petrol station after this in Iran. The place has atmosphere and the manager at one time was a frail old ex-schoolmaster trying to learn English from gramophone records. We had a pleasant little session while we each tried to polish up the other's language. Now there is a still frailer old man who seems to wrestle with the most elaborate accounting. An abacus which he twiddles seems to throw him into greater confusion and he looks sadder and sadder. I hardly dare order anything for fear my meal and drinks will be entered up in triplicate and then double entered. I did get a wintry smile from him last time as he recognized me as a third timer on the run in his era.

Once we could not get Skol! Stifling my panic, as it was an unusually thirsty run, I tried to stay calm. I never, ever take no for an answer anywhere, so I fenced a bit, warmed a bit, cooled a bit to weaken resistance and as I spoke Persian the barman at last said it was because it was the time of mourning – Moharram – for the Shia sect in remembrance of Hassan and Hossein, the grandsons of the Prophet. (See Chapter 18 for a description of this sect.) He added that he could slip the beer out at the back and convey it to the camper. There were two slips – he out of the back and a slip by us out of the front towards the camper at a smart trot. I can drink beer in any place, any time and in any position. My best guest night trick was to drink three pints standing on my head, but I was a little younger then.

There is another tip. There are shaggy dogs which bay at the moon all night, behind the restaurant. If you ask the manager, he will have them driven to a distance and kept there, so that you can sleep. Dog is Sāg in Persian. There is currently no charge for parking here and the truck drivers are beginning to use it in large numbers.

Marand. We do not normally leave the restaurant very early as we make a run of only three hundred and fifty miles – child's play on the good Persian roads and one could easily do more. Premium petrol is at the first station on the left as you enter the town of Marand, thirty-five miles from the restaurant. There is an inn just beyond, but its courtyard is very small. Marand sells good fruit and bread. If you can't see a bread shop (they generally hang up a piece outside), watch for early morning shoppers with flaps of bread over one arm.

Half-way through the town there is a roundabout at which you turn uphill for Tabriz. The centre is filled by a statue of the Shah on a high plinth of beautiful green marble. Every small town in Iran has one of these statues, generally in the middle above an island of flowers, grass, ornamental statuary and coloured lights.

As soon as you turn, the road becomes very steep with no room to charge it. It always comes as a surprise to me. I become lulled into a sense of ease by the wonderful roads after those of Turkey and forget that though the terrain is not so universally relentless as in the latter country, there are some very lofty surprises to come. I am somewhat testy and prone to blame my navigator unjustly for putting this hill in my path. At this the navigator snaps back that I am a curmudgeon. Although the hill is only six-and-a-half miles long with an alleged rise of six hundred feet, it seems to go on for ever.

Tabriz. One gets to the top in the end and continues straight on to Tabriz, the capital of the Province of Azerbaijan. It is worthy of a visit if you are making Iran the object of your journey, but if making for India it's best not to fall behind your schedule until you've passed Kabul, after which you can be sure of good weather. Azerbaijan has been so fought over by the Russians and British within human memory that its inhabitants are a little sour in their attitude to foreigners. Some of them are of Russian origin.

There is one of the oldest tiled mosques in Iran in the city, though only the Iwan or main entrance remains with a few blue tiles on it. It is fifteenth-century Seljuk – Turki, not Persian. When we went to look at it, the locals were very surprised and pointed out that there are two lovely *new* mosques up the road.

There is a fine covered bazaar, closed on Fridays and women visitors should be modestly clothed. The carpet centre is interesting. Tabriz carpets are made of fleece, not sheared wool and thus lack lustre. On the other hand they are knotted with a hook so the knot has to be on two warp threads in the Turkish style. It is now common in other parts of Iran to make the knots (which are normally tied by hand) on four warp threads. This produces a poorer, thinner carpet more quickly. If you can find one with the soft bloom of vegetable dye, then you have a fine carpet, as those of Tabriz are well thought of, but seek advice. Too many carpets all over Iran are now chemically dyed with analine, rouge d'orient, danyl and potassium chromate. The government tries to stop this, but it is difficult as chemical dyes are easier to fix and need less preparation. Owing to the demand in Iran by Americans, Germans and oil sheikhs one can probably buy a Persian or Turkoman carpet more cheaply in Britain.

As you approach Tabriz the road swings left past the airport: a lesser road goes straight ahead to the Tabriz Inn. There is a camp site on the other side of the city. I explored Tabriz years ago before these amenities existed and now pass straight through.

After the airport you cross a modern bridge which, thank God, has replaced the old rackety, one-vehicle-at-a-time one and go up a wide dual carriageway towards the centre of the town, looking out for switchbacks. As I remember it, speedbusters or sleeping policemen are mainly an evil of India and badly signed at that, but there are bad spots. There are petrol stations either side of the town.

The dual carriageway ends in a big roundabout and on the other side veer a quarter right over a narrow, hump-backed bridge ignoring all signs and directions from passers-by. We did once follow their advice and wound for hours through the back streets of Tabriz, ever narrower, ever more congested. Creeping at a snail's pace we became the victims of swarms of schoolboys who chivvied us like remorseless flies, knowing that there was no policeman away from the main streets. Never ask the way in the east except from a policeman or an obviously important and respectable citizen. Otherwise in order to get rid of you, people will say, 'Straight on', wherever you want to go. Few even know the name of the next town.

Continue straight on after the bridge and up to the second round-about – a very large one with a curious concrete structure like a pigeon loft in the centre. There follow the signs left to Teheran. This is one's first taste of Iranian town traffic. There are nasty little orange taxis which dart like fierce sticklebacks down the stream. They seem to be there expressly to balk one or get one into an accident. They pass on either side and stop slap in front to collect a passenger. They do sudden 'U' turns. They never signal. You will be absolutely O.K. though, pottering through at between ten and fifteen m.p.h. and keeping on the protected left side of the traffic stream if you can. Pedestrians are crazy. Traffic of all sizes, widths and speeds is crazy and children are cheeky, now the hippies have been here, though Iranian children do not have their Turkish contemporaries' exhibitionism and real bad manners. Stone throwing is rare and Iranians are by and large a friendly lot.

Having turned left for Teheran, go down an avenue or Khiaban through traffic lights and point duty policemen. The avenue becomes more ornate with elaborate coloured light arrangements, triumphal arches brightly lit at night, flower beds and statues. It widens into gardens with a roundabout. Such gardens are an innovation in Iran and do the country credit. It is cheering to see life becoming less squalid in this land of contrasting rough climates, though since the gardens are always at one end of the town they are not much used, being a long walk away. The statuary and plaster ornaments are often, it must be admitted, crude and vulgar. This may surprise you in a country which has so long and splendid a history of the arts, but it is exploding and so does not have time for self-criticism yet.

As always, the Shah's statue is prominently displayed and again on a plinth of lovely green and orange-veined marble found both in Iran and Afghanistan. It is said that the Shah's autocratic father who started to influence the layout of cities and towns laid his sword on the large-scale map of Teheran and said that the main avenue would go through there – and it was so! Certainly, all towns and villages have this dominating central avenue straight through them. How envious the Department of the Environment would be.

TABRIZ TO TAKESTAN – 268 miles

Mianeh and Zanjan. Leaving the city, follow the signs for Teheran and Zanjan. The next obstacle is the Shabli Pass (6,890 ft), a climb of over two thousand feet in twenty-two miles. It is not so fearsome as it sounds as the road is well graded. Dropping down again, you pass a beautiful lake on the left and continue up and down hill and later down a valley beside a river with small plantations of golden poplars and silver willows. This road leads into the gorge before Mianeh (a hundred and four miles from Tabriz). Here, one must again be on one's guard for a slap of side wind from a valley and for frequent tunnels. These are unlighted, so have your headlights ready. They are not long, but very dark, so don't forget to push up your dark glasses on entering them. Look out for sharp stones fallen from the roof. They can slit the outer skin of a tyre.

You can pick up super petrol at Mianeh and then drop down into the bed of another river. If you have a heavy vehicle, you will have to make a detour off the main road before getting to the petrol station.

It is not long, though rough. You then run along beside the new river and through a very long tunnel, lighted this time. Once through the tunnel you cross to the other bank over a modern bridge beside an old one with broken arches. The railway crosses the river too over a delicate and beautifully proportioned concrete bridge. You follow the course of the river for several miles, climbing imperceptibly and then swing eastwards (left) towards Zanjan, still climbing beside a tributary. Four miles the other side of Zanjan which is about eighty miles from Mianeh, you come at last to the top of the watershed and drop down towards Takestan, seventy-five miles away.

Zanjan to Takestan. Takestan is now on the signposts instead of Zanjan. Twenty miles out, look for the blue dome of the tomb of Sultan Oljaitu Khodabendeh at Sultanayeh, over on the right. This tomb dates back to the fourteenth century and is the first blue dome one sees in Iran. We once walked over to look at it from the horrific old road somewhat north of the present Asian Highway. It proved to be some walk as we had forgotten the rarified atmosphere which makes distant objects seem so near. It is very weather-beaten, which is a pity. It is always difficult to decide whether to restore an ancient building and if so, how much to restore it. These buildings were often crude in their bright paint when new and are better left mellow, but this hardly applies to the beautiful Iranian mosques which are all grace and lovely tilework. One thing is certain, modern skyscrapers and County and District Council buildings will not make beautiful ruins like these.

At last your straight road comes to a T-junction, some two hundred and sixty-five miles from Tabriz. The right turn is the road to Hamadan and of course Irak.

Hamadan. Hamadan makes a middle quality, longish pile carpet and its speciality is runners or long passage carpets and narrow border rugs. There is also an ornamental glass industry with vases of an unusual design with strange twisted necks in deeply lurid colours. Abu al Sennah's (Avicenna's) tomb is there and a modern jagged concrete memorial has been put over it which reminded me of the thing one uses with a lump of tow to clean out a shotgun. On the tomb itself there are two very fine Isfahan carpets. Their typical Islimi or snake design really refers to floral tendrils which curl in a loose coil. There is a memorial to

Esther and Mordecai of the ninth century which is also worth seeing, but as Hamadan is a side-step of a hundred and thirty miles, it is better to stick to the main route.

Takestan. The left turn goes to Takestan and half a mile down the road you can pull into a big service station with a restaurant and a hotel, three miles short of Takestan. It is a good night stop from Khoy and it is better to tackle Teheran in the early morning whether you are staying there or only passing through. I have made friends with the night-watchman who tucks us well in at the back in a small courtyard in the lee of the restaurant. It is sheltered and cosy and well back from the juggernauts' shunting. The drivers you meet here are a cheerful lot and do a minor trade in smuggled gallon bottles of Johnny Walker and gold cigarette lighters, always much prized in the east. The juggernauters do not like the swift buses with their pushing ways. One, a fair skinned Turk with wavy golden hair gleefully described to us how in a recent storm one of these buses, going too fast, was blown off the road. He continued with relish, 'They were all keeled'. We were offered coffee by these important and well-esteemed men. It was Turkish, sludge coffee, but we felt flattered.

TAKESTAN TO TEHERAN – 130 miles

Qazvin. If you wish, you can push on to Qazvin, another twenty-five miles. It has a hotel (Inn), but if you park there you have to rent a room for 800 rials (about £6.00) which doesn't make sense for a camper. There is no other particularly good place to stop between Takestan and Teheran and it is often difficult to pull off the road. However, make as early a start as you can from Takestan, still a hundred and thirty miles from Teheran. The rush hour there begins at half-past seven and parking places fill up early.

Going through Qazvin one used to be able to drive direct into the town as far as the large roundabout, on the other side of which lies the Qazvin Inn in an attractive garden. One then turned right and straight out of the town. Large vehicles now have to turn right down the first road signed for Teheran and out of town past the sugar factory. This road is being repaired, but was pretty awful last time we used it. If you are not too big, go the first way mentioned. Qazvin is a good place to stop and shop for food on the return journey and has some fine old mosques.

Karaj. The road to Teheran is straight and dull with increasing traffic as the day gets older. Sixty-four miles out of Qazvin you will see a large green signboard, pointing right to the Karaj Freeway. This is well worth taking, if they let you, as it is a good fast road while the road through Karaj town is rough and cluttered with very slow, beaten-up local trucks. You pay a toll of 10 rials at a kiosk. I said, 'If they let you', because the police sometimes have a rush of conscientiousness to the head and stop anything larger than a saloon car from using the road. It is always worth having a try as this attitude seldom lasts long.

Teheran. The freeway is just like any other motorway and gets you quickly to the capital. Leave it at the first exit to the city down a double carriageway and circle a huge roundabout with a vast inverted concrete shuttlecock in the middle. Jockey for lanes and go half-way round as far as the sign for the Teheran camp. The other road from Karaj comes in to this roundabout immediately after the one by which you entered. If you want to stay at the camp, turn off and follow the rather infrequent signs. I must warn you that it is not easy to find and when we once stayed there, we found it smelly. Some of the smaller hotels will let you live in their grounds, but that is a matter of luck. Frankly, we generally push straight on and spend the night near the Caspian.

Teheran is a vast oil boom city of little merit with an uncertain climate and extremely heavy traffic. You can't park anywhere, taxis are few and choose you, you don't choose them, as they pick up several passengers all going roughly the same way. It is worth going to see the crown jewels in the vaults of the Bank Melli on Avenue Firdausi. They are beautifully arranged by Cartier. There is also the Gulestan Palace which contains the so-called Peacock Throne, only it is a copy.

The covered bazaar has a central, well lit, round hall which is the centre of the carpet trade. The smarter carpet shops in the Avenue Firdausi display modern carpets of fine weave, woven on modern steel looms. These carpets have no souls. They are too exactly woven. A true Persian carpet is perfect because of its imperfections. But enough of this – I am not trying to sell you one. After the last war, the old dealers tended to go out of business and the modern proprietors know nothing about their wares.

Remember what I said about spares in Teheran. Land-Rovers and Leylands are assembled there and there is a Bedford agent. Most of the smaller cars are English Chryslers under another name. Mercedes are also assembled under the name 'International' while new ones, BMWs and Peugeots are driven in from Europe for sale in great numbers. There are ample VW spares and services.

Food is cheaper along the Caspian than in the capital.

18. *The Backbone –*
Teheran to the Afghan Border

DISTANCES AND TIMES

Teheran to Amol	..	..	..	122 miles	⎫ 1 day
Amol to Gorgan	..	..	..	125 miles	⎭
Gorgan to Shah Pasand	..	..		45 miles	⎫
Shah Pasand to Bojnourd	..	..		145 miles	⎬ 1 day
Bojnourd to Mashhad	..	..		170 miles	⎭
Mashhad to Tayyebat (the border)		..		135 miles	4 hours

If you haven't stopped in Teheran, Takestan to Amol, 252 miles makes a good run.

Mashhad to Herat (Afghanistan), 210 miles makes a good day's run as the border crossing is slow.

Total, Teheran to Tayyebat 742 miles.

TEHERAN TO GORGAN – 247 miles

Teheran is roughly half-way through your journey, but there are still some big obstacles to come. To carry the city, hug the old shuttlecock roundabout and three-quarters of the way round peel off down the Khiaban Eisenhower. This leads you naturally into the Khiaban Shah Reza which is an immensely long six-lane avenue, connecting with the Eisenhower at the 24th Isfand Square. The Khiaband Simetri leads off to the right for Isfahan (see Chapter 24) by Qazvin Square and the Khiaban Qazvin, Routes 6 and 7.

The fact that the Khiaban Shah Reza has six lanes does not stop taxis from trying to make it into an eight-lane one, by squeezing and jostling. The traffic intensifies after nine o'clock and is lighter again between 1.30 and 3 p.m., siesta time. If you are all going the same way, you merely have to keep bowling along with the merry throng. We don't give an inch and our rubbing strake is of metal-faced hardwood from which taxis shy as if from an overdressed salmon fly. Hug the left, along the flower beds, but keep a sharp lookout ahead for other vehicles leaving the avenue to the left and baulking you, which forces you to the middle lane for a while. You get the knack after a time and do not get put out if other vehicles skim past six inches away.

One is of course somewhat relieved to see the statue of Firdausi with fountains all round him in the middle of a large roundabout in the distance. He was court poet to Mahmoud of Ghazni and his war correspondent – in verse. When Mahmoud, the idol breaker, cooled towards him and left him penniless, he wrote the finest hate poem ever written about a master. Unbeknownst to him, Mahmoud relented and sent him money and gifts, but the emissaries arrived to see the poet's bier coming out of the gates of his house. (For more about Mahmoud, see Chapter 19.)

Firdausi's roundabout is about half-way down the Avenue Shah Reza. The Avenue Firdausi on which lie the British Embassy and the best shopping areas goes off to the right, and up to the left lies the Marmar Hotel where one can sometimes park and have a draught beer in the shabby 'English Bar' in which British salesmen foregather and complain about Iran in front of the English-speaking staff, all probably members of the secret police.

You carry straight on down the avenue Shah Reza through the slightly lighter traffic to the Shahnaz Square, quite unmistakable as it is large and the centrepiece is all a-gallop with improbable white plaster horses. The Khiaban Shahnaz runs off to the right and leads to the Khiaban Khorasan, the start of the alternative route to Mashhad south of the Elburz by Shahrud and Neishabur (see Chapter 24). You should continue to edge round the centrepiece and go slightly left up the Khiaban Mehran, signed for Ab Ali and Mashhad. This takes you straight out of Teheran, up into the mountains. There are good petrol stations as you leave, on either side of the road.

If one wishes to avoid the worst of the city traffic, one can carry on along the freeway from Karaj until it ends in a dual carriageway. Go straight on along this until you come to a T-junction. Turn left and carry on until you come to a large roundabout. Go round this and off half left up a wide street. At the second lot of traffic lights, turn right and down the wide road that runs at the foot of the hills above Teheran. This wide road leads at its end to the main avenue of Golhak. There at another T-junction turn right, go some way down the hill and at a large crossroads, turn left following the large sign for Ab Ali. You will later be signed into the Avenue Mehran and join the first route.

You now start climbing steadily. On every trip we have been baulked by refuse lorries which smell to high hell and are just fast enough to make passing too hazardous. Teheran dumps its refuse along the roads, every year farther out. It's easy in a big country where no one minds grub anyway.

In good weather as you reach the top of this rise which has just been remade in place of the excruciating switch-back from which we have suffered for years, look upwards for Mount Demavend, 17,000 ft, Iran's premier mountain. One can sometimes glimpse it coming into Teheran from the west and once we had a sheer unclouded view of it as we were coming home along the Caspian, but Caspian weather generally hides it.

The Haraz Pass. After this rise you disappointingly lose all your height and drop down again. Then you start climbing in real earnest to Rudehan, the ski resort and Ab Ali, thirty miles from Teheran. As you near Ab Ali you begin the climb towards the Haraz Pass and it is really steep. Soon the engine appears very flat and we usually get down into second gear out of five for a while. This is the shaley re-entrant with steep sides I mentioned before (p. 53). You approach a bridge, followed by a horseshoe and I always experience a sinking feeling as I look up and up as the road comes out on a spur above. After the horseshoe the engine gradually takes heart and as second gear rises to near 3,000 revs I go up into third which holds well with a little throttling back to spare and the revs are still under 3,000. I watch the road for any temporary increase in steepness and accelerate so as to carry it without losing momentum.

There is no need for anxiety in fine, snowless weather climbing this pass. Even in snow there is a snowplough to clear the way if you wait, and tow you if your wheels will not grip after stopping in a hold up. Near the top you go into tunnels designed to keep avalanches off the road. Then you are over. I have never had an accurate assessment of its height. There used to be a mark at 7,000 ft, but it was a long way down the climb. The A.A., I am sure, gravely underestimates its height at 6,800 ft. It appears substantially higher than the Tahir, though it is a better road of tarmac. Judging by the distance we climb after 7,000 ft, I think we have made at least another 1,500 ft, i.e. it is 8,500 ft.

Occasionally there is still an avalanche which closes the road on the Caspian side. If so, you are directed over another pass with rougher going called the Chalus. This lies west of Teheran and seems to get more sun and less snow, but otherwise is much the poorer route with a single-way tunnel some miles long, tentatively controlled by lights. Friends have recently reliably measured this as just on 8,000 ft and it does seem considerably lower than the Haraz.

Although the road is more difficult than that of the main pass, it is beautiful. You pass a splendid dam and lake on the way up and after some rather breathtaking hairpins on the way down from the top of the pass, the road runs beside wooded trout streams and delightful picnic places. At Chalus you turn right along the Caspian to rejoin the main road at Amol. There is a charming 'picnic' site half-way between these two places where one can park for the night. There are amplifiers in the trees to broadcast the song of the nightingales at the proper season. It seems these birds are becoming modern. I have, however, known this road badly damaged by floods and have had to drive part of the way along the Caspian beach. On another occasion, travelling in the other direction we found a large concrete bridge had been swept away and we had to turn back.

The Caspian. This route round by the Caspian does not seem the most direct especially when compared on a map with the one via Shahrud and Neishabur, but it is the main road to Mashhad, part of the Asian Highway and is paved the whole way through. The road was made through the Haraz Pass during the war in an effort to get supplies to Russia from the west. It is a fantastic engineering feat with many tunnels on the way down.

The top is some forty-two miles from Teheran and now you make the long descent to Amol, eighty miles away, standing back from the Caspian shores. The road is winding, so save your brakes and use your gears pottering down. The scenery is like the back of nowhere – all dull, shaley slopes, formidably precipitous. The mountain torrent down the valley is pleasant, but I won't bore you with a rather drab landscape. You should be watching each corner like a hawk lest some heavy vehicle come round towards you too close.

There is a good place to stop for the night down at sea level. It is ten miles short of Amol and two hundred and fifty-two out from an early morning start from Takestan. A lot of the run is steep and slow so one doesn't mind stopping early. If you have started rather early from Teheran and want to go farther, then the next good stopping place is a hundred and twenty-five miles ahead. Before Amol look for the signs for a picnic area on the right and pull off to park in the fenced-off bay below the road out of which a shady garden with benches, tables, W.C.s and water leads to the river edge. No one will bother you and there is a road patrol post across the road.

You want to use the rather short daylight hours to the full now, so next morning you should be out on the road by first light, all bright-eyed and bushy tailed. Nibble biscuits and hard-boiled eggs on the move later.

Skirt Amol by the by-pass which bears right off the main road towards Babol, twenty-two miles away. This brings you to a one-way bridge over the river. Turn sharp right to cross it. On the return journey, cross by another bridge a little higher up. After the bridge there are several bakers who work early, so it's not biscuits for breakfast after all. There is not much traffic on the road at this time. It is neither a beautiful drive nor particularly dull. The country looks central European and the people are sturdy and red-cheeked. There are horses everywhere, though now one sees tractors in the fields. Much of Iran's food comes from here, above all fruit and vegetables. The road across the pass is always cluttered by small vans carrying lettuces to Teheran.

From Babol, follow the signs to Shahi, Sari, Beoshar, Gorgan and Shah Pasand, where you leave the sea, which you can't see anyway. The route generally runs straight through the middle of each town after negotiating the inevitable formal garden.

Six miles after Gorgan there is the other place where you can spend a night – on a broad, grassy verge along a wood on the right. This could all be fast motoring were it not for the rough cluttered roads in the towns and villages where an erratic motley of vehicles is given a top dressing of the usual stickleback taxis. The pedestrians are more erratic still.

GORGAN TO MASHHAD – 360 miles

The Eastern Elburz. In Shah Pasand, a hundred and seventy miles from Amol turn left at the one and only roundabout opposite the police station. Petrol is a little farther on on the right and there is super, as there is all the way from Marand. Just after the petrol station the road forks right for Minoodasht and Mashhad – a direct, new route.

If you like you can keep straight on for Gombad-i-Kabūs (Gonbad-i-Kavus). It is ten miles farther round, but one of the few Turkish towns that the Russians have not swallowed in their steamroller progress eastwards through the Khanates and Bokhara. Here one can get rather attractive purple rugs of loose weave and longish pile. I doubt if you could still find the blood red, nomad rugs made by the Tekke tribe who lie or lay east of the Caspian and were called Tekke, or goat men, on account of their horsemanship in those foothills. Nor can you find the equally fine Salor camel bags with a ground of dark liver colour. I should imagine most of these staunch Muslims have been killed off. You can get Afghan replicas, but they are not as fine.

From Shah Pasand follow the signs for Bojnourd and Mashhad. There are many fast, pushing buses which take pilgrims to Mashhad. You can wear a green turban to show that you have done the pilgrimage to the shrine of the Imam Reza, the Shiah prophet. To go by luxurious bus seems a fairly easy way of getting your pilgrimage done.

The Shiahs and the Sunnis are the two main sects of Islam. The Shiahs believe that the Khalifat descends by appointment and succession and the Sunnis prefer the principle of election. The Shiahs are largely found in Iran and in some small enclaves in Pakistan, N.W.F.P. The Sunnis make up the rest of the Muslim world except for the small sect of Ismailis who follow the Aga Khan. The Sunnis are very orthodox and are not supposed to drink alcohol. The Shiahs take a more liberal view and are devoted to their own saints, the Imams, of whom the holiest, the Imam Ali-al-Riza, the eighth of the twelve, is buried in Mashhad. His tomb still stands, but that of his great enemy and contemporary, Haroun-al-Raschid, Caliph of Baghdad, who was also buried in Mashhad has disappeared.

Ten miles after Minoodasht which is about twenty miles from Shah Pasand, the road swings right up a long valley and back into the Elburz Mountains to the Mohammed Shah Reza Wild Life Preserve. You climb up a beautifully wooded valley with a small stream. Later, the valley widens out and leaves the trees behind. There are, I believe, fair numbers of Ovis and Markhor still on the heights and possibly some leopards. There are numerous picnic places in the Shah's forests where one can pull off for the night. They are marked and one must not halt anywhere else. Some friends of ours tried a site and were joined by a bear half-way through the evening. I'm not sure who was most startled. There is super petrol at Robatgharbil, seventy-five miles from Shah Pasand.

The Bojnourd Passes. About forty miles short of the town there are a couple of parking places in the valley before you climb the Bojnourd Passes, on the right near a little river. The four steep passes do not present a great problem now as the road is tarred all the way. Although the climbs are long, they are not difficult. One year, before the road was remade, we met snow on the highest pass. We seemed to be gripping well when we came to a solid block of pilgrim buses. The occupants were sitting apathetically doing nothing and freezing. There was nothing for it but to bully and cajole them into pushing their own buses over this small snowy crest. In the east gentlemen don't get out and push, so it needed a lot of persuasion though it was dangerously cold just to sit. Once they'd got the idea the buses moved well to cries for help and strength from God. I helped and called with the best, but as soon as a gap was formed, hopped into our camper, drove through and was off on my way. They were all quite pleased and expressed their gratitude and continued to push through. It only needed the great organizing brain of Mutt.

Bojnourd. This is the final place to get super before Mashhad, a hundred and seventy miles away. Get it from the big petrol station six miles on the other side of the town where there is plenty of room. Just beyond the petrol station there is a large picnic area where one could stop for the night. We never have, as it always seems crowded and noisy. Nine miles farther on there is a disused road on the right below the main road and parallel with it. It makes a good place to stop on the return journey if one has started from Herat in the early morning.

Mashhad. The drive to Mashhad is straightforward and is across a wide plateau, now under cultivation for the first time. Reasonable sugar beet is already being milled there. Fifteen miles short of the city you pass the turning for Tuş where Firdausi (see p. 116) is buried. You can go round Mashhad by the Asian By-Pass, rather than stopping there, if you wish. Super petrol is only at the big station near the airport on the other side of the city. Drive straight in on the main road as far as a really large roundabout with inner and outer road rings. Go half-way round it and take the road signed Torbat Jam, which is near the border. Another road leads off three-quarters of the way round, marked Down Town, the route to see the sights. There is a camp in Mashhad, signed in from the road to Torbat-e-Jam, soon after the roundabout.

Mashhad is a rewarding stop. The two most splendid mosques are the shrines of the Imam Reza (twelfth century) with its unusual golden dome and, more magnificent still, the mosque of Gauhar Shad, a famous empress, descendant of Tamerlane (fifteenth century). This latter is one of the finest examples of Muslim architecture and tile work in existence. When we visited Mashhad, we were not allowed to approach close to it. Now the Shah, growing stronger, has prevailed upon the Mullahs to allow tourists to visit it. Women must wear a chador, which can be hired from nearby shops. It is a light voluminous covering of head and form, nearly always in some drab, small pattern to discourage feminine vanity. Men must have their heads covered. Seek local advice as it is still a touchy subject. We stole a fair photograph shot from the window of the museum nearby when the guard was not looking. Walking about the city on its broad pavements we saw so many interesting and differing types of tribesmen. It is a very fine eastern city and its avenues of poplars and cool cypress-edged gardens spread each year. The police are particularly helpful here and think nothing of leaving their point to hop on a moped and guide you. Alas, like so many other posts of prestige the British Consulate no longer exists.

MASHHAD TO TAYYEBAT Afghan Border – 135 miles

The Asian By-Pass round Mashhad seems to go for a long, long way through rubbish tips and shanty settlements on the edge of the city. At last, however, you should slow up near the airport to turn in to the petrol station, just opposite the Information kiosk, where they never seem to know anything. If you are travelling in the winter the place to find out about road conditions in either direction is the petrol station where truck drivers congregate. Fill up here with premium and put as much as you can in every spare container. I dislike carrying petrol like this, but there is no more premium until Pakistan a thousand miles away and Afghan petrol is so awful that it is vital to help it out.

After this, follow the signs for Neishabur and Fariman. This road has recently been realigned the whole way through semi-desert country with fine mountains standing well back from the wide valley.

Sang Bast. At Sang Bast, twenty-two miles out of Mashhad, the road divides in two. One goes off to Neishabur, the burial place of Omar Khayyam and the other over the river and the railway towards Fariman, your next destination. The Iranians do not rate Omar the tentmaker's poems very high and say that it was only Fitzgerald's translation that enhanced them. They prefer Saadi and Hafiz. Once upon a time businessmen and others when faced with a decision used to open their books of poems at random to find the answer to their quandary. We used once to use the bible like this in Britain.

There are places where one can pull off the road for the night after Sang Bast. If you do this, you can make an early start, picking up normal petrol for the last time at Tayyebat, five miles short of the border.

The Border. Aim to arrive at the newly built frontier post on the Iranian side, which is very splendid and more convenient than the old one, by eight o'clock, half an hour before its official opening. Officials are frequently late, but I think by arriving here first one gets a flying start. This border is always crowded and you might find a bus load of travellers later on in the morning who greatly gum up the works, as do those travellers who are improperly documented or uninoculated. At least one establishes rapport with the minor officials before the great men of the border roll up in their smart bus. They may put your passport before their master more prominently than those of others when he has pulled himself together. If you speak a few words of the language, they certainly will.

You hand in your passports to the police together with the little pink forms and your passports will eventually be stamped with huge stamps when all your details have been laboriously copied into the vast ledger. You go through the same procedure with the customs for the car. Iranians are always extremely polite in what appears to us a flowery way, so don't stint your greetings. To ask how the children are getting on is always a winner in the east, anywhere, any time. Have a photo of yours and you'll really hit the jackpot. If you haven't got any, borrow some.

19. *The Backbone – Afghanistan*

Islam Qala (the border) to Herat	..	..	..	75 miles	2 hours
Herat to Kandahar	..	..	..	360 miles	1 day
Kandahar to Kabul	..	..	..	308 miles	1 day
Kabul to Tor Kham (the border)	..	..		150 miles	

The run from Mashhad to Herat would fill a day. Peshawar in Pakistan is 40 miles on from Tor Kham and a good halting place. Leaving Kabul in the early morning, you should be in Peshawar by late afternoon. The border takes a long time and parts of the road are bad.

Total mileage in Afghanistan 893 miles.

ISLAM QALA TO HERAT – 75 miles

The Border. Having left Iran you run along an excellent road through a sort of no-man's-land for about a kilometre towards a splendid board welcoming you to the 'Front' of the new Republic of Afghanistan. It may be a bit of a struggle to get through as far as the back. Once upon a time the struggle began here as there was practically no road and what there was led through a stream into a sea of mud. We even had to put our small diesel at the bank of the stream on one occasion when the ford was full of capsized petrol tanker. The gallant little beast just struggled over.

Your first 'Welcome' nowadays is a barrier across the road and a sentry who looks earnestly at your visas and passports, upside down, before he lets you in to the promised land. Then you come to Islam Qala (Quila), a huddle of low buildings either side of the road with a dusty garden in the middle of it.

You are directed down the left fork to the customs, but don't look at your guide, look at the potholes. The Afghans are always changing the rules of the game, so you may be told to stop in front of the customs' building, round at the side or in a malodorous little area at the back. Wherever it is, you have to avoid gaping craters in the ground which never change from one year to the next.

You will find the customs officer in a tiny cell, generally crammed with young western travellers who have probably stayed the night at the hotel (*sic*) on the border. Last time we went through, most were in varying types of fancy dress or artificially aged jeans. There was a fuzz of beard garnishing the top area. Oh, how I wished the younger generation weren't so tall. My five foot ten got nowhere. But at last due to some pushing and swaying a gap appeared, and I saw the inundated clerk and he saw me. I hailed him heartily with the setpiece Pushtu greetings, Pushtu being the official language of the country. They begin, 'May you never be tired, O Master Official.'

He replied automatically, 'May you never be poor' (see Appendix II).

We both went through the whole routine and he then put down his pen, looking up in surprise at a westerner speaking Pushtu at all. Down went the passport he was handling and he got up and came round through the crush to shake hands, which is also the custom. He led us from the Black Hole into another room and gave us the forms to fill in. Then excusing himself to the crowd, saying he must have a cup of tea, he came out with us to look cursorily over the car. After the farewell ceremonial we were through the customs.

As I suggested before, money changing has to be played by ear, but this is the moment when you will be approached, if the bank is not open (see Chapter 4).

You take the vehicle carefully back over the potholes and wheel right into the health office, beside the customs, for the inspection and stamping of your certificates. Then you motor over potholes, into potholes and out of potholes round the central garden to the other side of the road and the passport office, pestered by boys asking for money. Somehow scrape up a few coins to buy them off while you are inside if you value your paint. The passport police office is quite large, so there is more room for my expansive Pathan greeting. The large uniformed figure here is most friendly and always delighted to find his own signature on our passports from previous visits. He will gaily flick out your visa forms, so laboriously filled in England and drop them into the wastepaper basket.

Then at last after more ledger filling, you can move up to the next barrier, but you cannot go through yet. Car insurance has to be done at the government office just beside it. Without this and it doesn't take long, the sentry will not let you through. He inspects all your documents, turning them round and round and breathing heavily as you champ at the bit and the camper paws at the ground. At last he will be satisfied and dreamily raise the barrier.

The Road to Herat. 'Smack went the whip, round went the wheels.' You speed along a good road across desert country. It should be innocent enough, but there are two long Irish bridges that can be tricky. One year, travelling the other way, we were churning across one of these bridges which was in spate with a duststorm blowing like a plume through the same gap as the spate. This reduced the surface to moving mud. We followed a local truck as the markers on the road edge were submerged. A wise precaution, I felt. I could not have been more wrong. The truck stopped with a jerk. I had a split second decision to make – to stop and stick, or squeeze by, risking going over the edge, which was hidden. I was lucky and in passing peered into my 'guide's' cab. Above it was a thirty-five gallon drum of water which had split, cascading its contents over his windscreen and blinding him. Later, going through cutting after cutting with sand building up, I misjudged the depth and caught my right wheel on a pile of it. We whirled round, leaning over and over – I looked down at the navigator below me – and then we slowly righted. A passing farmer was relieved of his spade and in the same motion a fifty Afghani note pressed into his unresisting hand. I dug us out quickly, returned the spade and drove on. How wise old Mutt had been to design his vehicle with all the weight low down.

The first toll is some twenty miles from Islam Qala. The charge is not exorbitant – about 30p. – and one is glad to pay it for good roads. One does resent getting out of the vehicle to find the clerk rolled up like a chrysalis in some hole or corner hiding from the rigours of the weather.

I always enter Afghanistan with many memories – those of twenty-six years ago when I was Military Attaché in Kabul and travelled the country widely, including a foot-trek, skirting Nuristan whose fair people are, probably wrongly, supposed to be descended from Alexander's armies and across the little-known Nawak Pass to Anjuman. Those were happy times though the non-alcoholic official stag parties were dull as my ambassador, a fussy little man, would play bridge for hours and we could not leave before him. In recent times the beautiful Afghan women have at last broken the purdah which Amanullah tried to pull aside prematurely. When staying at the Embassy a few years ago we were introduced to some of them. Their jade green eyes were in some cases quite magnificent. Like so many Muslim women who have stepped into the outside world, they are making up for lost time in education and responsible positions.

Herat. Some twenty miles before Herat, once the centre of such turbulent history, you hand in your ticket at another toll barrier. This is simple – the soldier at the barrier takes it from your hand at the window and returns half to you. Keep this half to show next time you buy a ticket. It saves argument as to your rating and will have your number already on it in Arabic figures.

Then look for what appear to be five tall factory chimneys far away on the right. These are the few remaining minarets of Gauhar Shad's mosque and ecclesiastical school which an absolutely soulless bounder, Eldred Pottinger, had blown up. It is the same Gauhar Shad who build the mosque in Mashhad. She ruled here after her husband's death and is popularly believed to be buried near the minarets in the once-splendid tomb with a melon-ribbed dome like those of Samarkand, built by the same dynasty. The tomb is neglected and gradually falling to pieces, but it is still beautiful. The fine, tiled mosque in the centre of the city dates from the thirteenth century, but has been fully maintained and restored. Each tile replaced has been faithfully copied. I would not describe it as a great piece of art as the tiled design is small and fussy with no overall concept. One can buy very good quality donkey bags in Herat, which make excellent cushion covers, in fine knotted carpeting in the Turkoman tradition.

Eldred Pottinger, a young Irish Artillery Officer, arrived in Herat from Kabul in 1838 a few weeks ahead of an invading Persian army. He wore eastern dress and was travelling for pleasure as did a remarkable handful of British adventurers of those times. It was an entirely private undertaking except that he had leave from his masters, the East India Company.

Although at the time the British were not adopting an active anti-Persian or in effect anti-Russian posture (for the Russians were behind this Persian move, as usual stirring up trouble where they could), one can see where Pottinger's sympathies lay. In character he was the romantic ideal of Victorian days being tall, strong, religious, courageous and industrious.

Far from withdrawing at the threat of Persian invasion he taught the Herati Afghans to make defences and by his example encouraged them to resist so strongly that their efforts forced the Persians into a long-drawn-out siege.

Unfortunately from the point of view of future lovers of beauty he blew up several of Empress Gaur Shad's minarets in front of her religious school in order to clear a field of fire, so that now only five remain.

If you want to know more, do read Arthur Swinson's excellent *North West Frontier* (Appendix III).

Skirt the town past the petrol station as far as the T-junction with the road coming down from Russia on the left. Turn right, signed for Kandahar, ignoring the policeman who will try and wave you slap into the bazaars of his beloved city. The road runs round the edge of this old town to the new town that has grown out of the old one, on the other side. It is pleasant with conifers – a relief after the desert. On the far side, turn left on to the Russian concrete road for Kandahar and drive along an avenue of firs. The best petrol station is two hundred yards on on the left. The pumps at the first one have an odd way of measuring petrol and the second claims to have a choice of two brands.

Petrol Stations. Here you must watch your change and work the sum out for both parties. A favourite trick is to palm a large note requiring change and show one of the same colour and less value, claiming you still owe them money. Never let your money out of your hands until the change has been handed over. They have too a way of not flicking the indicator back to zero when they start filling. A threat to appeal to the police whose methods are rough and ready will usually work if you have trouble. The attendants slop the precious liquid on the ground a bit as do all easterners. One gesticulating wildly with the hose gave his companion an eye bath once and there was more gesticulating. Petrol here is not expensive as the government keeps the price down.

Hotels in Herat. Half a mile farther on, on the left, is the Russian built Herat Hotel with a pleasant garden and friendly manager. He has a smart assistant who used to puzzle us until we discovered that he is half Afghan and half Japanese. The other two assistants are red-haired, half Afghan and half German. Parking under the huge car-port costs forty Afghanis a night and you can get a tolerable meal and cool non-alcoholic drinks as well as tea. This is a good centre for exploring Herat and there are many other hotels of varying degrees of respectability, mostly in the new town mentioned above.

Mechanics. There are two fine mechanics, known as the Brothers, who live in this new town. They are also called Hajjis as they've been to Mecca and keep open house to beggars. They once showed us great kindness and gave us the most skilled help. While we sat on a bench, anxiously watching over our ruined ewe-lamb into which they were trying to breath the kiss of life, beggars used to file through the workshops and collect small coins off the Hajjis. There were no thanks, but we remembered that in the east things are often the other way round. They were doing the Hajjis a favour, for the giving of alms is more blessed than the receiving.

HERAT TO KANDAHAR – 360 miles

The road soon starts climbing and leaves the conifers behind to go over a pass of 6,000 ft. The mountains stick up only a little way above the surrounding uplands, largely shaley desert. It is severe, fine scenery. The mountains take on weird shapes and look like prehistoric monsters crouching guardant. The earlier part of the journey is enlivened by mirages of lakes and trees in the distance, always on the same stretch, but the bare hills themselves change colour as the day advances and are never monotonous.

Farah. The toll is fifty miles out of Herat and the ticket is handed in seventy miles farther on, as you turn in to the extensive service and hotel (sic) area near the Farah Rud (River). There's plenty of room to spend the night tucked in round the first bend, in a garden area, if that suits your plans. The hotel has no food and hot cold-drinks, but tea is available and fair. It is innocent of poisonous milk, but there is lots of sugar. I'm not a tea-bag man myself and my friends wouldn't recognize me if I were, but they aren't here to watch me pour from a pot with a little sack in it. How odd to find Thomas Lipton here when one would expect tea in bricks from China, brought in on long camel caravans. The hotel dogs demand the moon all night to the detriment of sleep, but one has to expect that anywhere.

Dilaram. The road continues through the bare, fine uplands with jagged peaks and crags, but falls gradually to Dilaram, eighty-three miles farther on. There is a sort of hotel there and a hand-winding petrol pump. The toll is just across the river and you have to scramble up a hillside for the ticket. The road then climbs over the not particularly noteworthy Daruga Pass, twenty-seven miles on and drops down to Girishk on the Helmand River.

Girishk. The damming of the Helmand by the Afghans has been a source of friction with Iran since it flows over the latter's borders into the Seistan Desert. There is petrol at Girishk on the right of the road just before the river and a blind beggar just beyond to whom we always give some coins for luck.

Maiwand. The road now rises slowly on to a high plateau and you continue at an average of 3,000 ft. You soon pass Maiwand far on the left. A few low hills in the dust haze mark the scene of one of the two defeats of the British at the hands of the Afghans in all the battles fought between them. While I drive, keeping a careful eye on the thermometer needle, I realize how that little force must have suffered. In July 1880 acting on an incorrect report that there were only a few Afghans at Maiwand, a small flying column with light artillery was sent out from Kandahar to deal with it. They found a large Afghan force of more than twenty times their number astride the only water hole and covering it with heavy artillery. The British force was unable to dislodge the Afghans and thirst and wounds led to a complete defeat. Anyone who has known the agonies of real thirst, as I have myself, will know how that force suffered. They marched in tight red tunics in the heat of the day which was in itself bad tactics. Wounded men tried to limp back to Kandahar and a great wounded Highlander dragged himself as far as a village. For three days he called out for water before he died. He was in full bonnet, kilt and all the regalia and the Afghans cowered in their mud huts, too afraid to go near him. 'Will ye no come back?' I always feel sad thinking of this man dying alone in a foreign country and of all the other simple private soldiers whose bodies were left for the jackals and to what purpose? Everything for which they fought and suffered has been thrown away by succeeding generations.

The Seistan Desert. Over on the right there is a vast pink escarpment stretching parallel with the road for miles. One suddenly realises how big it is when one sees trees and villages like small black and buff sprigs and grains at its feet. This is the eastward edge of the Seistan desert. Some say it moves a mile a year eastwards. Perhaps this is an exaggeration, but it is certainly much closer than when I first saw it twenty-six years ago. I believe there is no way of stopping this high edge of pink sand on its all-engulfing advance. One looks at it with awe.

Kandahar. Simply because it's a change one is glad to drive into another avenue of conifers leading into Kandahar. The best petrol station is on the right as you come in, after a double row of stalls. They do not try and cheat you. I hope you have been keeping your eyes open for stone throwers. From now on you will have to be doubly careful as the worst areas lie ahead.

The name Kandahar is a corruption of Alexander, or Iskander, the form more familiar in these parts. The remains of Alexandria Arachosia lie to the west of the modern city and the country must have looked very much the same two thousand years ago. There is little left to mark his passing except perhaps for the great platform, the Chelzina, later adapted by Babur as a place for a victory inscription.

Kandahar lies at 3,400 ft and has always been an important town at the junction of trade routes. If you stop the night, try the Kandahar Hotel. It is a depressing place, but they let one park for the usual fee and it is guarded by a police post. It is no noisier than the other hotels which are as sleazy as their semi-foundered European occupants. I must warn you that the place looks as if it had never been cleaned and the sanitation is worse than you can imagine. The Afghans are not natural hoteliers, though usually very friendly.

Much of the town has been modernized though some of the old shrines have survived. Some of the antique shops are interesting and one can still pick up a piece of Gardiner china here and there. The factory was established in Russia for the Empress Catherine by two Scotsmen, father and son and produced delicate china for the Russian and eastern markets until 1917. They made rice bowls, tea services, dinner services and occasionally figurines which are their most famous product – there are some in the V. & A. They don't turn up here, as representing the human figure is against the Muslim religion. You will find designs of medallions of flowers on a white oval ground, against a background of deep crimson, blue or very rarely, green. There are also purely Russian patterns with a lot of gilt and some Chinese ones. The mark is in red with the Russian Imperial Eagles above St. George with the name Gardiner in Arabic characters beneath. The rare green pieces have a big gold 'G' as well. Good pieces are stock-marked. This china is still made, but is instantly recognizable by its poor paste and clumsy workmanship. Being much prized in Afghanistan and northern Pakistan it is not cheap.

If you are in trouble – and I was once when I blew up the engine – the Hajji Kaya Serai is the place to go. It lies just off the main road. Ask for Mohammed Reza Khan who is an extremely nice man, still youthful and much respected here. The serai is all small motor repair shops let into the walls where great skill keeps museum pieces on the road with antique tools. Mohammed Reza Khan did the almost impossible to save us, far beyond the daily task and at small cost to us.

If you can avoid it, as I said in Chapter 10, don't buy bread in Afghanistan. Things are just that bit too fly-blown and the flour is very coarse. It is better to gnaw a bit of Iranian bread, probably as hard as leather by then and step on the gas.

To get through Kandahar, drive straight in past the Indian and Pakistan Consulates and the Kandahar Hotel, all on the left, up to a big crossroads with a roundabout. The roundabout is off to one side but chunter round it, and go left. At the bottom the road swings right and straight out of town. Near the airport. it forks right to Quetta (see Chapter 24) and left to Kabul with no side turnings.

KANDAHAR TO KABUL – 308 miles

Powindahs. Although it is all uphill, you can get a move on along this American tarmac road as traffic is light. You pass through various villages and travel across a wide plateau along the Tarnak River. In October the nomad Powindahs or Kuchis are on the move. They tend to use the road, which is I believe forbidden. Camels are nervous beasts and can swing across the road suddenly – their owners are usually armed with rifles. Be careful and wave in a friendly manner. Some of the men are tall and handsome, but not quite the paladins of John Masters's books – John, whom I knew, is a romantic anyway. The women age quickly in this hard life and seldom wash – water is too precious. Their wealth is in their anklets and coin ornaments, though some nomads used to be rich as they lent money to timorous Indians farther south and had unpleasant but firm ways of getting their money back with good interest. Nowadays they are not even allowed into Pakistan. Their low black, camel hair tents are known as kirries and don't camp wild near them. Powindahs are answerable to no one.

Kalat-i-Ghilzai. The toll is forty-five miles out of Kandahar and forty-three miles beyond this is Kalat-i-Ghilzai. Its fortress is unmistakable and can be seen a long way off. The petrol station (your first Russian petrol) is on the other side of the village, on the right. Don't let truck drivers bounce you in the queue. Be firm and they will give way with a laugh, but be friendly. Their friendliness can swing suddenly to ill-temper as with many volatile easterns. The best implement you can use is a kind of open friendliness and simple, almost facetious humour. I was talking once to a wild-looking gang armed to the teeth and when they asked me where I had learned Pushtu, assured them that I had picked it up fighting their fathers. It was the joke of the season and they fell about laughing – we were friends for life after that.

The next petrol pump is at Mukkur, but it is a battered old thing. There was once a rest house where I remember staying nearly thirty years ago. It is now an official headquarters.

Ghazni. Your toll ticket is handed in fifteen miles short of Ghazni and two hundred and fifty out from Kandahar. Ghazni, once a large city, is now only a fortress, bazaar and hotel. They fake and weather 'ancient' Bactrian coins and make poshteens – embroidered sheepskin coats with all the hair inside together with its invincible smell, in the bazaar itself.

The simple tombs of Mahmoud of Ghazni and his father, Sabuktaghin, are near the fortress. There are two towers of decorative brick on the far side of the town. They have always been supposed to celebrate Mahmoud's triumphs. Modern archaeologists think that the towers are probably minarets like that recently discovered in Ghor, but more worn down by the weather. There have been important excavations in this area in the past ten years whose results are largely in the museum.

Mahmoud, son of a Turkish nobleman Sabaktaghin by a slave girl –

a common occurrence – inherited his father's firm base at Ghazni in 998 A.D. Soon to be known as a Shah or King, he strengthened his empire, using Ghazni as his capital and centre point for expansionist wars into Central Asia alternating with seasonal raids in India. His great generalship enabled him to shuttle rapidly from one territorial extreme to another.

His raids deep into India were really bank raids to replenish his coffers to pay for the good life, his armies and his wars. At this time Hinduism was experiencing a golden age of great elegance, wealth being centred on great temples. Such raids, even those by the Mughuls and others later, just left the peasantry to carry on. They did not really affect them to the degree one might have expected.

The greatest of the temples was Somnath near Patan in Kathiawar on the Arabian Sea. Fifteen thousand Brahmin priests served there and five thousand beautiful girls on the staff sang and danced to the glory of the gods. Mahmoud was soon at the gates of Somnath – which he eventually took back with him. The priests fought till all were killed, with fifty thousand other inhabitants of the city. The temple was full of gold and silver-encrusted and encased idols. Mahmoud had these smashed and stripped; was he not known to all as the Idolbreaker to the glory of Islam? The centrepiece of the temple was an idol which appeared to be suspended in thin air and was obviously the greatest treasure of all. Mahmoud sent a spearman behind to see if there was anyone or any device holding it up. 'No, it's just floating, O great smasher of idols.'

Mahmoud not to be outdone by the Hindus whom his more advanced scientists despised, called forward a smart party of these Arabs from his entourage. They fiddled about with the idol and decided it must be of iron and the canopy above it of 'loadstone' so constructed that the stone exerted an equal force from all sides and kept the idol suspended in a magnetic field. Some of the stones were then removed from the top and the idol began to tilt. After a little more tampering it crashed to the ground and from it gushed cascades of rose coloured pearls, bigger than peas. There scattered was the richest treasure of all.

I have pieced the story together from the writings of Al Kazwini and Mahmoud's court poet, Firdausi whom I mentioned in Chapter 18. Of course I have filled it out and read more too, for while working for an exam I had to translate this and other tales from the Shahnameh which had already been put into Pushtu with Arabic script adapted for it by Sir George Roos-Keppel, once Governor of the N.W.F.P. Until then Pushtu was not a written language. I mention this because I want you to read a little, imagine a lot and repeople old places.

As you approach Ghazni the fort stands out prominently; at its foot there is the sleazy bazaar and on the western spur, mud dwelling houses of no distinction. What a comedown from Mahmoud's heyday. In those days the city walls were twenty miles in circumference. In the foreground is the well-signed hotel with an arid garden in which campers can park. On seeing me for the first time the manager resorted to his prayer mat. The responsibility of scaring up a hasty meal for us was just all too much. Fortunately we could provide for ourselves, but for a while he kept returning to his mat if I approached and followed me anxiously out of the corners of his eyes as his lips moved mindlessly muttering prayers. All I wanted was to have the usual scrounging pariah dogs driven away.

The petrol station is visible from the hotel and if you win across the potholes, they will hand-crank you some Russian petrol. The main road to Kabul is straight ahead and swings right at the foot of the hills away from the town. Unless impeded, you can get a bit of a run up to start on the very steep shortish pass which rises eventually to 9,000 ft. The toll is twelve miles out and the ticket is handed in eleven miles from Kabul at the foot of what appears to be the steepest bit of all, effectively stopping a run up. The country between the first and last passes is wide and undulating. Whichever way you are going, it gives the impression of being uphill. You pass walled villages and fort-like dwellings, an occasional stream and small fields painstakingly cultivated. At the top of the last pass you look down a steel hill towards Kabul (5,900 ft) in a hollow surrounded by hills, some fortified, like the historic Bala Hissar.

Kabul and Afghanistan. Kabul is a jumping-off place for expeditions to various parts of the country. As the best travelling seasons are late spring, summer, or early autumn they should probably be a separate undertaking.

The scenery of Afghanistan is grand – there is no other word for it. Much of it is very barren, so that a tree or a stream is of enormous value. Parts of the country such as the Koh-i-Baba (N.W. from Kabul) are high enough to produce the changes in colour as the light changes that are a feature of the Tibetan uplands.

Apart from scenery and the varied tribes, archaeological remains are perhaps the greatest interest. I have always thought of Afghanistan as the Cockpit of Asia, even as Belgium is that of Europe. Numbers of conquerors have passed through it, fought over it, settled in it and founded rich civilizations, from the days of Alexander onwards. It is not easy to get permission to visit archaeological sites since there are well-grounded fears of pilfering by foreign visitors. However, the tourist can usually go to Bamian, Band-i-Amir, Balkh and the overrated Mazar-i-Shariff without difficulty. There is a good road northwards to these places through the Salang tunnel, supposedly the highest in the world and built by the Russians.

Bamian contains two splendid Buddhas, each over a hundred feet high, carved out of a cliff face, as well as cave monasteries. Band-i-Amir is a series of horse-shoe shaped lakes formed in limestone with brilliant clear water. Mazar-i-Shariff has a fine Blue Mosque of the fifteenth century – I personally think it looks like a municipal bathing establishment. Beyond it lies Balkh, 'The Mother of Cities', once the centre of the Barmecide sect who specialized in illusion. There is little of it left now beyond the ruined walls and mosque. Unfortunately someone decided there was treasure there and the whole place was devastated by treasure seekers.

There is a road from Mazar-i-Shariff going south-west to Herat which we have not driven over, but friends recently wrecked a Range-Rover on it. A lot of it is sandy and cut across by tributaries of the Oxus which wash away the shoulder.

There is excellent trout fishing in the rivers north of the Hindu Kush, communicating with the Oxus or Amu Darya. I believe I still hold the record at 13 lb 14 oz caught in the Anjuman Lake in the north east. I had some identified in England years ago as ordinary, natural brown trout. A former ambassador, one MaConnachie, believed them to be a new species and got them named after himself.

The Afghan ruling clan of Persian origin is the Durani, derived from the phrase, Dur-i-Duranis, or Pearl of Pearls. I say ruling clan since the present President and architect of the revolution is also a Durani, first cousin to the former king.

Although Persian is most used – a Persian that is much more clipped and less affectedly sonorous than that of Iran – the government is encouraging a change to Pushtu. This is the tongue of the Pathans in the south who also lie across the border with Pakistan. As Afghanistan claims this territory both in theory and rhetoric they try to foster Pushtu which they now call Afghani. That is why they are extra pleased when you speak it, even if their own VIPs are slow to change.

Kabul has been modernized and has good shops, even that little outfitter of mine, Marks and Spencers. Wealthy Pakistanis used to shop here until the change of government and its anti-Pakistan propaganda made visits impossible for them. The streets, once deep mud, are tarred and the traffic rather heavy. There is a camp to the north of the town, but it is not well supplied with amenities. The Afghan government has dropped down on the drop outs, but there are still junkies about, male and female, ready to do anything for dope. So long as opium is grown openly, I do not see how they can be got rid of. In the spring the fields round Jalalabad are gay with these lovely flowers, pale pink and white in large plantations.

It is possible to camp or rather park in the grounds of some of the hotels such as the Ariana. The British Embassy is in a lovely garden compound surrounded by the pleasant houses of staff and officials. I did once go back after twenty years to see the almond trees I had planted. They were doing well. Although one would be assured of a warm welcome, I think it wrong to intrude on the Embassy staff who are not there to look after casual visitors, and we content ourselves with very happy memories of our time here with the children in a healthy climate.

KABUL TO TOR KHAM (Pakistan border) – 150 miles

If you do not stop in Kabul, take the most traffic-free way as follows: drive into the town down the dual carriageway and turn left round a roundabout at the first traffic lights. There is petrol here, but it is a badger's muddle and I once found when topping up that they claimed they had put in more fuel than the tank would hold. The next petrol is at Sarobi, forty-five miles on and watch your change. If you can't last till Pakistan, fill up at Jalalabad ninety-five miles from Kabul. If you filled at Ghazni and still have some Iranian on board, you should be all right.

Continue down the road to a T-junction and turn right up a slight slope, past the Intercontinental Hotel and the road up to the Bagh-i-Bala, the palace of Abdur Rahman. That formidable old ruler at the end of the nineteenth century had the salutory habit of baking bakers who gave short measure in their own ovens and shutting thieves up in cages on the scene of the crime. He died in this palace and it was left empty for years, haunted perhaps by his terrifying ghost. Now it has been tidied up and turned into a restaurant where one can get a reasonable meal in these romantic surroundings.

The road drops again past the Embassy gates. In my mind's eye it used to stand on a rise in splendid isolation, four miles out of Kabul on a road that heavy bombers could not have damaged more. Now I see there was no rise and it is surrounded by a huddle of town houses on a tarmac road. Go down this road towards Shahr-i-Nau (Newtown) and come to a large open space with a point duty policeman in the middle. Three-quarters of the way round him go down the street to the second lot of traffic lights and turn right for the Kabul River with the former palace gardens on the right and the Ariana Hotel later on the left. At the river bank you will see a clock tower. Go round this and off to the left, braving the stench of the river which is a sewer, and bump hideously over potholes. The road gradually leaves the river and keeps straight ahead, past the radio station, a number of factories and barracks.

What an improvement this route is on the old Lateband Pass. This gorge road is spectacular and a major engineering feat by the Americans. The Kabul River waxes and becomes a heavy torrent, checked at intervals by hydro-electric installations. This was the scene of the only other British defeat in 1841. Demoralized by bad leadership from an incredibly old general who had tried to avoid the command, the column – suffering from cold and confinement in poorly sited lines – stumbled down the gorge, hampered by women and children as well as innumerable camp followers. In spite of a safe conduct it was steadily whittled away by attacks from large Afghan forces, and in the end most of the troops and all the camp followers died. Left without food or clothing the latter resorted to cannibalism. Dr Brydon managed to get to Jalalabad, but the few Europeans left were taken prisoner. Many of them ended up at Bamian whence they were rescued by a detachment from the relieving column under General Sale. His wife was among the prisoners and her journal has given us many details of the disaster.

Sarobi. As the gorge widens out you climb a steep, short shoulder and drop down to Sarobi, near the big dam across the river that has formed a large lake here. There is a toll to pay and a hotel where one can stay in the pleasant garden that is often crowded and noisy.

After this the road continues along the river, but generally the valley widens out and there is substantial cultivation where before the construction of the dam there was wasteland. Twenty-six years ago we used to climb in and out of nullahs, round broken bridges, scaring big monitor lizards out of our way. In the distance, near the river, you can see groups of palms, popularly supposed to have grown from date stones spat out by Alexander's men.

Jalalabad. This was the old winter capital and there is petrol on the left as you enter the town. You carry straight on past pleasant gardens with cypresses, many of them hotels. After passing a few bazaar stalls, turn right at a small roundabout and down a crowded street with shops and stalls on either side. There is a branch of the Da Afghan Bank near this. Shortly you come to another roundabout with a point duty policeman and turn left round him down the road to the border. This road is crowded with pedestrians, flocks, camels and swaggering tribesmen. The school on the left is notorious for stone throwing, if for nothing else. I think they have special classes in this art.

The last toll gate is some twenty miles out of Jalalabad. As you go along the road under the shady tamarisks it is difficult to see the very deep switchbanks since the general surface looks harmless in the patchy light and shade. It is advisable to drive very slowly till one gets out into a more open avenue and to be careful of this treacherous surface every time you come under thick trees. The road has been allowed to deteriorate during the last few years. Damming the Kabul River has brought greenness and crops to this hitherto desert country. However, no one has yet persuaded the tribesmen to start re-afforestation on the predominantly bare hills. Chopping down trees for fuel over hundreds of years has denuded the land.

Dakka. This post is eight miles from the border and officialdom has one more fling before you can escape. You have to leave the road and drive into a large compound where you and your vehicle are chattily inspected by a military guard before you are allowed to go farther. It is a quite cursory inspection which seems to be promoted more by boredom and curiosity than anything else. The object of the manoeuvre is totally obscure.

The Border. As you are a camper, ignore the string of lorries on the left and drive up to the steps of the customs house on the right. These offices are roomy, unlike those of Islam Qala and the formalities are as described in Chapter 4.

You then toil into another building to show your passports once again, this time to the police and yet again your details are laboriously entered up in the huge ledger in Arabic script. I always wonder what eventually happens to these ledgers and does anyone ever look through them again? I suspect everything ends up in the wastepaper basket like one's visa forms. Then at last you are free, a chain is unlocked and a pole rises.

20. *The Backbone – Pakistan*

DISTANCES AND TIMES

Tor Kham to Peshawar	..	..	..	40 miles	1½ hours
Peshawar to Rawalpindi	..	..	..	106 miles	⎱
Rawalpindi to Lahore	..	..	..	172 miles	⎰ 1 day
Lahore to Wagah (border)	..	..	..	12 miles	½ hour

(Traffic is very slow and heavy as you leave Lahore and the road bad).

Total distance through Pakistan 330 miles.

TOR KHAM TO PESHAWAR – 40 miles

The Border. As you cross from Afghanistan to Pakistan, you switch to the left of the road and are greeted by a Pakistan Scout (Transborder Policeman). I avoid greeting the Guard Commander in Pushtu nowadays. I did it once and when he saw my old Scout badge which I have on every vehicle for nostalgic reasons, he turned out the guard, though I protested that I was old, retired and had no standing any more.

The welcome at Tor Kham is very warm indeed and a score of Pathans will wring one's hand in the likable, man-to-man way they have. There is an atmosphere of smuggling in the air and much more on the ground. Get one of the sentries to keep an eye on your car while you are in the various offices. If it is locked, nothing is likely to be stolen, but for some reason they like to prize off one's G.B. sticker, possibly for smuggling in another car I am told, but how escapes me.

Once more your passports will be stamped and details filled in in a ledger. Although Pakistan is no longer a member of the Commonwealth everybody behaves as though she still were, and holders of Commonwealth passports are put through quickly in a separate ledger. We ourselves talk of old times and famous names of my time on the Frontier and find their descendants among the staff, for this is a kind of homecoming for us. Green tea, that most refreshing of all drinks, spiced with cinnamon and white cardamom is ordered. We sip it, trying to get through it without appearing to hurry. Although we do wish to get on to Peshawar, it touches us to be given such a warm welcome.

After the passport office there comes the Khyber Road Toll of six rupees, for as you have guessed this is the mouth of the famous pass. Remember it closes at both ends at sunset. Then you move your vehicle to squeeze in by the customs office thirty yards up the road to get your carnet stamped and your possessions cleared. Any traveller who is friendly and forthcoming will be kindly treated, especially if well combed and brushed. They get too many of the other sort nowadays. You do not have to fill in currency forms, but you are not permitted to take Pakistani rupees out of the country with you. The Habib Bank is just opposite the customs.

The Khyber Pass. Clear at last, you then crawl up a black, stony bluff in a series of horseshoe bends, remembering to stick to the left but keeping a wide eye open for the lovingly and gaudily decorated trucks which bounce recklessly down towards you. Above on the left are the large garrison hutment barracks of Landi Kotal. Away on the right is Char Bagh, another historic defended post near the site of an almost extinct gold mine. Then you pass through a post at a road block, round the corner and up through a very narrow, cluttered bazaar. There are Ford V8 1936 tourers still plying there, but now they carry sixteen or more passengers inside with some in the boot. The older they are, the harder their life.

The bazaar which extends in some depth is a huge black market area. The Pakistanis have been rather clever in their relations with the Pathans of the buffer tribal strip between themselves and Afghanistan. The bazaar is in this tribal strip which is known as tribal territory, guarded by the Scouts and administered paternally by Political Agents. After tentative attempts to stop widespread smuggling which is difficult to do in hilly terrain with tribes who have one foot in either country, they have finally bent to the pressure and permitted this smuggling and the forming of black-market areas in the buffer strip. They know this suits the Pathan character and keeps them happy, because they are avaricious. The Pathan wants money the easy way only, and he got it in the past by raiding and extortion. This, I believe to be one of the reasons why he has been relatively quiet until now.

The customs outpost through which you came is by-passed by

convoys of donkeys and men portering the smuggled goods. As you
came up the pass you may have seen a hundred donkeys carrying two
truck tyres each. They have simply walked round the custom post and
rejoined the main stream of foot and animal traffic that goes up the pass
on a special road beside yours. You can buy Rolex watches, English
cloth – you name it, we Pathans have it! Friends in Peshawar will offer
to get one anything one needs through 'a little man they know'. I
remember once being invited up from Peshawar by a local chieftain for
one of those huge mutton pilaus with all the fixings in his fortress home
and afterwards being taken to a hillock above the border to watch the
continual stream of contraband making its placid, unconcerned way to
the market. There one can also buy large cakes of 'charas', a type of
hemp which is sold openly in great quantities for smoking, but I wouldn't
recommend it.

Chunter carefully through the bazaar, go over the head of the pass
and begin the long descent. The pass is great in history, romance and
valour, but it is physically not gigantic. Still, it has been the gateway
forced by invader after invader making for the lush plains of the
Punjab. It is in fact rather small as passes go, compared with those
you have already crossed, being only 3,500 ft. Small stone-throwing
boys are at their worst, unrestrained by smiling adults – 'It's only the
lads' high spirits!' Higher still when they add catapults as is now the
fashion.

On the valley side above the road are the crests of British and Indian
Army regiments who fought there or acted as garrisons. The crests are
still in good repair and I can still see one group of four, of which by
coincidence I have worn two myself – one British and one Indian. There
are too the remains of concrete barriers and pillboxes built during World
War II against a possible German invasion from southern Russia – a
new form of steamroller. Up on the more commanding heights are small
fortified posts or permanent pickets. I have often scrambled round them
in the past on inspection.

You come next to the pumping station, another post and the water
supply system for the larger forts. The sepoys used to mispronounce it,
'Pimping Station'. Then half-way down you will see Ali Masjid, a fort
which has seen many a battle, but which became untenable with the
advent of the long range rifle. Tribesmen could rake the walls from the
surrounding heights. After this you pass big, pink brick Shagai Fort

flying the flag of the famous Khyber Rifles (Scouts too, such as I served
with in Waziristan so long ago).

My memories race over the youthful days when first married and
the need to jockey for leave to go down to Peshawar for the occasional
week-end with one's wife. This was sparingly granted since someone
had to stay on duty. We had a Commanding Officer who had the
sadistic habit of going in to lunch, over which he seemed to take a
deliberately long time, while the leave-book lay on the hall table awaiting
his written approval or veto. With my car loaded up with shot gun,
bedding roll, spaniel Cholmondley and bearer, I would champ and
mutter, growing hungry but not wishing to go into lunch for fear of
appearing to accept a possible refusal. If leave was granted, how I
covered those miles to lovely Peshawar where my wife and I had been
married. I claim I held the record for this run. One simply hurled down,
each bank neatly cradling the car round.

It was in Shagai that I heard the reedy voice of that gullible and
insular man, Neville Chamberlain, announce that we were at war with
Germany in 1939. One was not exhilarated, but thankful that we were
going to face up to reality at last. Would one get a family station as one
had been hoping? Would one – Hell, not for many years.

You then approach Jamrud Fort which lies across the exit from the
Khyber. Here one hands in one's toll ticket and gets a further scrutiny
from the police. You are not yet free of the police as opposite Islamia
College, now a University, you will be stopped at another and new
police post. Your carnet is inspected again. They will tell you they have
to check for smuggling as there are other ways of getting a car through.
I suppose this is possible if it were dismantled and humped bit by bit.
I wouldn't put it past the smugglers who would in any case find it more
fun to do it like this than to obey the law. Were it actually driven over
by any other route, it would arrive in the Peshawar Vale as scrap.

Peshawar. Peshawar is not far from Charsadda, once the capital of
Gandhara and a very old city. The Vale is lush, watered by the Bara River
and now more and more by the damming of the Kabul River at Warsak.
The old orchard area of Tarnab is greatly extended and the Bara Plain,
once a dull expanse of shale to our jaded eyes from the fort, is green with
wheat. Formerly it must have been still more lush before wood cooking
fires and a growing population's demands consumed the forests. Not so

very long ago the Emperor Babur hunted rhinoceros there and I shot snipe (forty-two years ago), so things are going down. Rhinoceros hide used to be ploughed up by farmers and is still so tough that the round Afridi shields are made of it. So good is the water in the Bara River that Babur and his successors had it carried by runners to Delhi for their personal use. The quality of water is always of the greatest importance in the east.

Peshawar was the scene of some of our happiest days. The great feature of the Cantonment is the Mall, four miles long and flanked by fine flowering trees and well-kept gardens. In spring the scent of orange blossom is heavy on the air and doves are almost deafening. The snows of the Safed Koh form a backdrop to the scene. Tongas trot up and down the Mall hopefully looking for customers and little motor-cycle taxis dart about, gorgeously ornamented, obviously the pride and joy of the owners' hearts.

You can stay at a hotel or at the Dak Bungalow (Resthouse) where you can camp at the end of the Mall. The hotels are: Deans, grim and expensive besides being the oldest; Jan's, the smugglers' paradise where at least the food is good; the International which is used by many travellers and is less expensive; and lastly the Intercontinental. This was not yet open last time we made the journey, but will presumably be just like all the other Intercontinentals all over the world. These are in the Cantonment and there is also the Park Hotel on the edge of the city – new and clean, but noisy and little room for parking your vehicle. There are several Chinese restaurants on the Mall and our little visit to Mr Fuji at the Hong Kong has become a seasonal one. Bland Mr Fuji says, 'Leave it all to me,' and he does wonders.

Alexander's main force came down the Khyber under the command of Hephaestion while he did a flanking movement through present-day Dir and Swat. The whole area is full of Graeco-Bactrian remains and there is a fine collection at the Peshawar Museum.

A visit to the City as opposed to the Cantonment is rewarding, for it is the true ageless past. Perhaps you should enter as the camel trains still do through the Kissa Kahani Gate (Gate of the Story Tellers), so called as traders from all the great uplands of 'The Roof of the World' used to pass through and bring news and ask news. There were no newspapers then – perish the thought. Although tales and rumours swelled step by step along the dusty mountain tracks so that they rang with drama under this portal, they were probably more true than the tales of the modern press who have to feed their gore-thirsty and accident-hungry readers. Minstrels still sing about great deeds to the accompaniment of the rabab.

There are copper-smiths whose musical beat rings out from a row of shops. There are fruit stalls and sign boards where the pox doctor advertises his nostrums to cure old age. Many years ago I used to be invited to dine in the City and one would pass through great doors like those of a baronial castle and feast off Gardiner china. The dining room would be impartially decorated with splendid carpets and cheap toys from Japan.

As Peshawar is nearly six thousand miles from our home base I usually get the car serviced here, at Peshawar Motors (Vauxhall and Bedford). They give one a great welcome there and one of the mechanics wears an automatic pistol even when working under the car. He is one of the many Pathans who have a blood feud and must be quick or dead. I also plan to get the vehicle serviced here for the homeward run as they already know it and their work is good. There are agents for most of the other makes either here or at Rawalpindi.

PESHAWAR TO RAWALPINDI – 106 miles

Nowshera. You will now be travelling on the old Grand Trunk Road. The surface varies and the tarmac is still rather narrow so that you may have to leave it for the dusty or muddy area at the side in heavy traffic. Beware of the fierce and accident-hungry buses and the maelstrom of tongas, taxis, pedestrians, trucks and what-not as you skirt Peshawar City for the open road. Twenty-five miles out you drive down the central road of another large military cantonment, HQ of the Pakistan Armoured Corps: Nowshera (Newtown) has none of the charm of Peshawar, though there are fine shady trees there and lovely deep-verandahed bungalows built many years ago by the Public Works Department against the heat. Half-way through, just after a level crossing, there is a road left across the Kabul River over a narrow bridge that is shared with railway trains, turn by turn. This is the road to Swat and Chitral through the military station of Mardan, once the regimental centre of the famous Guides. We went there some years ago to visit my own old regiment whose centre it now is and they kindly asked us to stay the night. We slept in their guestroom under bedspreads that had been made for HM the Queen and the Duke of Edinburgh when they visited Mardan and the Queen unveiled a memorial to a cousin, killed serving with the Guides.

The road on to Swat which is worth visiting if you have time goes through the Malakand Pass and Chakdara. My father commanded the post many, many years ago. We often go up to Chakdara for a day's fishing at the fishing lodge on the river there. We try conscientiously for Mahseer, but have never been there yet at the right time. The expedition usually turns into one of those wonderful eastern picnics that are really gatherings of large families and their friends, all busy cooking kababs and variously disporting themselves. There is nothing so vulgar as sitting on the ground – chairs and tables and plenty to drink are the order of the day.

Attock and Taxila. Another twenty-five miles on from Nowshera you cross the Attock Bridge over the Indus which separates the North West Frontier Province from the Punjab. Above is the junction of the Jhelum and Kabul Rivers and the current is very strong. The Mughals had a bridge here, long since swept away and there is a great fort up the side of the hills that is still in use.

The next place of interest on the way is Taxila and you should visit it if you are new to the country. In my opinion the ruins and museum show Buddhist art at its best. Indian art had not then acquired the pneumatic quality that one sees in the Apsaras and the gods and goddesses of later times, when stone was turned into human flesh rather than bone. Often repeated representation seems to lead to over-stylisation and in Indian idols this flesh has become inflated rubber in stone. Taxila is best reached by the road to the left two miles after you have passed through the town of that name, shortly before the Nicholson memorial which stands above a small pass. Don't take the earlier road signed from the middle of Taxila as it is clogged with traffic.

Islamabad. About a hundred miles from Peshawar you will see the avenue for Islamabad, the Rah-i-Kashmir that leads eventually to Azad Kashmir, on the left. This city has the makings of one of the most harmonious of eastern capitals. In the lee of green hills and with an artificial lake it is developing sensibly without too much hurry, which brings brashness with it. The area has trees and is well watered with a fine hillock overlooking it nearby with ornamental trees planted by visiting rulers. Other ornamental trees on its slopes blend gradually into the forest to knit the scene together cleverly, for young cities tend to have little general cohesion. The residential quarter is well laid out in a grid of wide roads and avenues in rectangles. I am glad to say the new British Embassy there has dignity, unlike the South Bank Exhibition egg racks thrown down haphazardly on the ground which lamentably house the British High Commission in Delhi.

Islambabad itself is not yet ready for tourists since it has only one hotel and few eating places. If you wish to stay in the area for a while, there are hotels at various prices in Rawalpindi, some six miles away. Flashman's is old-fashioned and most of the rooms depressing, but the food is very fair and there is a good car park. The Intercontinental is like all Intercontinentals, and probably the best bet for campers is Gatmels Motel on the Lahore road where the prices are reasonable and you can stay in the gardens.

RAWALPINDI TO LAHORE – 172 miles

If you do not turn aside to Islamabad the road to Lahore is straight through 'Pindi Cantonment and is well signed. The first stretch is through the tumbled hills of the Salt Ranges and has a peculiar charm reminding one of old prints of the sub-continent. The road is very bad and narrow in places, but is gradually being improved.

You cross the River Jhelum just over seventy miles from 'Pindi and pay a small toll at the beginning of the splendid bridge. After this you are in the flat plains of the Punjab – agriculture for miles, but the road is shaded by fine trees. Noisy parakeets skim overhead and doves make way reluctantly as they rise off the road. You run through various towns and villages thronged with traffic, preoccupied pedestrians and over-loaded tongas (pony carts) lurching perilously across your path. The journey is still complicated by aggressive and custom-hungry buses. Lightly built on diesel-engined chassis, they dash about all over the place and hog the road.

Lahore. There is another toll to pay as you cross the River Ravi on entering Lahore. This is a good place to spend the night before crossing the border to India. Many hotels will let you stay in their grounds. If you don't already know Lahore it is well worth spending some days, going over the Fort, the Mughal Shalimar Gardens, Jehangir's tomb, the Jamma Masjid which is very fine and the Montgomery Gardens, named after a former Governor of the Punjab, not the Field Marshal. There are said to be trees from every corner of the former Empire in these gardens. If you have not already got your frontier crossing permit, this is the place to do this. It usually takes about an hour, at the local office of the Ministry for Kashmir and Home Affairs.

Lahore is not a difficult place to find one's way through. After you cross the bridge mentioned above, bear round to the right and carry straight on for a considerable way. Do not on any account turn left near the Jamma Masjid with its white dome and pink and white walls and minarets, or you will congeal in a maelstrom of traffic in the thronged city area from which it is very difficult to extricate yourself. Mutt did it once, but only once.

Keep straight on from this cross roads, leaving the Masjid on your left, until you come to a large roundabout where you go half right through a narrow neck and carry straight on again, along a broad, sometimes double, carriageway until you come to a crossroads by the Telecommunications Centre on the right. There, turn left, past Kim's Zam Zama – the great gun round which he played – and along a wide street past European-style shops. The better hotels lie on the shady double carriageway in the Civil Lines beyond the shops and in the neighbourhood of the Governor's House.

To the Border. Leaving Lahore for the only crossing point into India, go down this road as far as the Canal, which actually marks the boundary of Lahore Military Cantonment – a very important place – I was born there. Turn left before the bridge down the canal bank past nursery gardens and railway quarters, over several level crossings until you meet a broad road coming across the canal. There, turn left again and follow this road to the walls of the Shalimar Gardens where you turn right and follow the signs to Wagah, the border with India, twelve miles out of Lahore. The last petrol station in Pakistan is on the left, just after the Shalimar Gardens, but it does not have premium, which you can get as you enter the town. I top up my tank here, anyway, as the petrol is cheaper and of better quality than in India.

Wagah. The approach to Wagah border post is winding and switch-back. The post itself is less cramped than some you will have gone through and both sides are open from 8.30 a.m. till 5 p.m. seven days a week. Nowadays it is not crowded. On the Pakistan side police and customs are in offices side by side on the right of the road. The formalities are as usual and you hand in your road passes there. All this done, you set out for India round a curious screen of reeds designed to hide the two countries from each other, and the goal of your journey is at last in sight.

21. *The Backbone – India*

DISTANCES AND TIMES

The Border to Delhi	..	..	320 miles	1 day

Route 1, Delhi to Madras via Hyderabad – 1,481 miles

Delhi to Agra	..	..	124 miles	4½ hours
Agra to Gwalior	..	..	73 miles	3 hours
Gwalior to Saugar (Sagar)	..	..	187 miles	7 to 8 hours
Saugar (Sagar) to Nagpur	..	..	244 miles	9 to 10 hours
Nagpur to Hyderabad	..	..	304 miles	11 hours
Hyderabad to Bangalore	..	..	343 miles	12 hours
Bangalore to Madras..	..	..	206 miles	7 hours

Route 2, Delhi to Madras via Indore and Poona – 1,603 miles

Delhi to Gwalior	..	..	197 miles	7½ hours
Gwalior to Shivpuri	..	..	70 miles	3 hours
Shivpuri to Indore	..	..	228 miles	11 hours
Indore to Dhulia	..	..	162 miles	6½ hours
Dhulia to Nasik	..	..	100 miles	3 hours
Nasik to Poona	..	..	123 miles	4½ hours
Poona to Belgaum	..	..	210 miles	8 hours
Belgaum to Bangalore	..	..	307 miles	11 hours
Bangalore to Madras..	..	..	206 miles	7 hours

The journey from the Border to Delhi can be done in a day, but you are advised to stop for the night at Karnal, 75 miles short to avoid arriving in a strange city late in the evening. Average speed on this run is not much over 30 m.p.h. This applies to all motoring in India with its heavy, slow traffic and narrow bumpy roads often passing through congested towns.

THE BORDER TO DELHI – 320 miles

The Border (Attari). There tends to be rather more form filling on the Indian than the Pakistan side of this border, but one gets through it in time. Passport and customs offices are in the same building. The formalities are as usual except that you have to sign a form promising to re-export your vehicle, and a currency form. The branch of the

State Bank of India does not generally open before ten o'clock, which is a bit galling if you have made a great effort to get to the border early.

Amritsar. Once you are through, drive straight on for Amritsar. Unless you want to stay there to see the Golden Temple of the Sikhs, continue through the town along the old Grand Trunk road. If you stay, there are several quite good hotels of which the Imperial is the most reasonable. To pick up the Grand Trunk road, drive into the town until you come to a fork in the road. Take the left-hand one (one way only) as far as the first roundabout, where you turn up right over a bridge over the railway. On the far side of the bridge, turn left down the road and out of the city.

Don't try to get to Delhi in a day from Lahore. It is too far and the road too slow. I would suggest stopping for the night at Karnal some seventy-five miles short of the capital.

The Grand Trunk Road. This by-passes Jullundur, Ludhiana and Ambala, the only big towns on the route which is clearly signed, either for one of these towns or Delhi itself all the way. The road varies in surface from very fair to fairly bad, but improves a little after Ambala, about a hundred and twenty miles out of Delhi. It is a lovely, tree lined, ancient highway through flat agriculture. You can see the old Mughal cos or two-mile marks from time to time. They are tapered, round pillars set up by the road, the pediment generally decorated with advertisements. Tractors are used for the fields but also to take trailers full of gaily dressed people to market. It is amazing how many cram aboard. This is an innovation. They do impede the motorist, but not so much as the bullock and even slower buffalo carts which they are replacing in this, the more go-ahead, fertile, Indian half of the Punjab.

For some extraordinary reason, India spends quite a lot of money on sanctimonious warning boards beside the road, written in dog-English, as comic as inappropriate. These warnings are directed at reckless drivers and would therefore be more appropriate if written in Hindi – ninety-five per cent of the population cannot read English. The standard of driving in the sub-continent is not good, but it will never be improved by remarks such as, 'Safety Saves', 'Safety First, Luck After Wards', 'Accident begins where Safety ends' and 'Drive Carefully Your Children

Are Waiting At Your House'. I find the last remark more than a little threatening.

Truck drivers try to be helpful, but their vehicles are often slow and grossly overloaded so that they are loath to pull over to one side to let you overtake or even to pass them in the other direction. They are rightly afraid of overturning on the sharp lip of the road where the tar ends and the dust or mud begin. They have to overload because the police exact unofficial tolls from them on the road – often on the grounds that they *are* overloaded – so they motor round in a vicious circle, if you get me. Look out for the Indian private owner-driver. He has all the bad driving habits you can think of.

Karnal. As I said above, this is the best place to stop for the night. There is a small place on the left of the road, called the Tourists' Paradise where one can camp for a small fee beside a lake. There is a snack bar, WCs, etc. and if you wish for a passable meal you can walk round the lake to the Whistling Teal restaurant – it's not very grand by European standards, but clean, and the waiters are pleasant. It is largely patronized by huge Indian families from the town of Karnal. Stopping here for the night means that with an early start you can arrive in Delhi, fresh and comparatively untried with the whole day before you for finding your feet.

New Delhi. The one place of interest you pass through after Karnal is Panipat, the scene of all north India's more important battles. It is of more interest for that fact than for anything to be seen there, since there are no memorials or important features to be seen as the road runs through yet another crowded, overgrown town.

I must confess that we have a two-day halt in the luxury of the Ashoka Hotel in Delhi, but then we've earned it after all these years. We always wash and change in the hotel's large car park before booking in as one is back in the smart world. I think the Ashoka is probably the most comfortable hotel in Delhi and it has a fine car park, which others haven't. Moreover, one is next door to the Shanti Path, flanked by Embassies and the Nehru Gardens – the one area you can really walk without being ploughed down as you generally are in India. Although is is government-owned, it is expensive and so are all the first-class hotels here. There are many cheaper hotels, an International Youth Hostel and camps, so everyone is catered for.

The Ring Road. To get to this area of Delhi, take the ring road round it to the west. It is a long and crowded way over an execrable and smelly road, but other ways are liable to land you slap into the Old Delhi bazaar where you will congeal with the crush.

It takes off to the right just before Delhi after the first collection of shanty stores and the truck service area. It is a wide turning with a divided carriageway which is a bit shabby and sketched out, but you know you are all right because immediately as you turn you can see a hump-backed bridge, over which you go. Carry straight on past the Britannia bread and biscuit factory and then gradually bear left on a wide sweep for a long way, crossing side roads and hooting and cajoling your way through the most varied types of transport you could imagine. Go very slow, but hold the initiative. It is a tedious ending to a long journey, but you are certainly seeing life, millions of it. You just potter along from pothole to pothole, sticking to this route through the stench of rubbish tips and eventually pushing through a growing bazaar. Then skirt round the military cantonments which lie to the right. You can even see the brick tower of the old British garrison church and a charming pink sugar confection – a Hindu ashram, or place of religious contemplation – in the Rajputana Rifles Regimental Centre. The garden and the whole lines are spotless. I have been there many times in recent years, as I commanded the Third Battalion in Burma many years ago.

Then you reach a large roundabout with low green iron railings. Here, turn left up the Sardar Patel Marg and after half a mile or so, right down the Panchsheel Marg. There is sometimes a policeman at this turning and failing this you will see one of the strange concrete sculptures with which the Delhi Municipality has 'beautified' New Delhi. The Marg takes you past the American Embassy on the right with modern 'jali' (lacework concrete screens) and on the other side of the Shanti Path past the horrific British High Commission on the left. Continue straight across the Shanti Path to the next roundabout which is surmounted by what can only be a giant thumbscrew in concrete. Turn left and a little way down, right into the Ashoka Hotel.

Camps in Delhi. The Nehru Camp, north of Delhi is rather far out, and the best for the purpose of visiting the capital is close to the Kashmir Gate. You will see the signs just after you go through the gate, coming from the north and having ignored the ring road. The camp is quite roomy and there is hard standing for campers which is most important in a dusty eastern town. There are hot showers and reasonable WCs and a shop where you can buy eggs, bread, etc. It is quite easy to find your way to the High Commission and Connaught Place, the chief shopping area, from here. You will find that many of the friends you have made on the way will turn up at this camp. The charges are very modest – four rupees a day for a camping vehicle and one and a quarter a day per person.

Shopping. Before you leave on further adventures, Delhi is an excellent place in which to stock up. There are good grocers and chemists in Connaught Place. Very good fruit is obtained near the railway-station, and meat in the Gol Market. Cold store chickens and edible bacon come from the grocers. Besides the bread at the Ashoka already mentioned you can get good cakes at Wengers in Connaught Place. Cooking gas comes from the Burma Shell or Indianoil installations on the Rohtak-Hissar Road which you will have crossed if you took the ring road.

You can get Indian manufactured textiles, brasswork, etc. at the Government Emporium on the Jan Path. Shopping for silver ornaments can be done in the Chandi Chowk in Old Delhi, and while you are there you can have a Bohemian type of meal at the Moti Mahal, famous for its Pathan-style food. The big hotels have good restaurants which are not very expensive. Other eating places tend to be just that, eating places.

Seeing the Sights. You will have to decide from the guidebooks what ancient monuments you want to see, but one place well worth visiting is the Delhi Zoo, not only because it has lovely gardens where you can walk, but because it is well laid out. Tigers lived in large open spaces here long before they did in Regents' Park. Besides the famous white tigers from Rewa you can see Tiger Jim, whose 'desperate' charge has figured in many an intrepid wild life photographer's films and books.

It's not a bad idea to leave your camper securely locked in camp and in the charge of a nominated camp follower and use a taxi for your forays. This is the common practice. Unless you are a midget van, the

Ambassador taxi (a by-gone Morris Oxford made under licence) will do a better mileage per gallon and will act as your guide too. It is better for it to have an accident than you. New Delhi is well laid out and the traffic not nearly so bad as Istamboul or Teheran, but parking is difficult and Old Delhi is hell. Taxis are plentiful, run on meters and are not desperately expensive.

DELHI TO MADRAS (Route 1. 1,480 miles; Route 2. 1,603 miles)

This section is chiefly for the benefit of those who intend to continue their journey to the Far East or Australasia. If you intend to fly either from India or Nepal, and many do, you can dispose of your vehicle for a small sum only – see Chapter 4. If you intend to go by land, then you must take to the sea, which sounds rather Irish. It is not possible for political and security reasons to cross Bangladesh or Burma, nor do the roads built during the war in the latter country still exist. The best route is from Madras to Penang or Singapore by ship. Make your arrangements for this well ahead in England through the Shipping Corporation of India, Lime Street, E.C.4. These arrangements must be confirmed on your arrival in India. Do not leave it to chance as proceedings in that country are slow and uncertain. From Singapore you can go by sea direct to Fremantle. If you have time, try and visit Thailand. There is a road from Singapore to Bangkok and the roads in Thailand itself are generally reported to be good. Besides the charms of Bangkok the country is beautiful and there are some fine wild life reservations. One word of warning – you are not allowed to live in campers in Singapore.

There are three possible routes from Delhi to Madras:

1. Down through Agra, Gwalior, Hyderabad and Bangalore.
2. As above, but turning west at Gwalior and continuing through Indore, Poona and Belgaum to join No. 1 at Bangalore.
3. Down the east coast from Bhubaneshwar. I would not recommend this as it is long and thick with slow traffic. The surface is generally poor and there are tiresome obstacles such as the Godavari and Krishnar Rivers and the port of Vishakapatnam.

Refer back to my general remarks about camping in India on p. 14 and forward to Chapters 22 and 23 where holidays in India and the Indian character are discussed.

ROUTE 1 – Delhi to Madras via Hyderabad and Bangalore, 1,481 miles

Delhi to Agra – 124 miles. Leave Delhi by the southbound National Highway No. 2. To reach this drive past Humayun's tomb, cross the ring road and carry on down the road to Mathura (Muttra). This is a four lane road that narrows to two lanes after the above town. I will leave the sights of Agra to the guide books.

Agra to Gwalior – 73 miles – (National Highway 3). The road is narrow and you are continually crossing and recrossing the railway. Level crossings are a curse all over India as they are numerous and the gates are always shut at the appointed hour, regardless of whether the train is late. You may have to wait a very long time, pestered by street sellers and crowded by bicycles. Nearing Gwalior look out for the State Railway – almost a miniature, built by the grandfather of the present Maharajah. He delighted in driving his own trains until he ran over a cow and it cost him a great deal of money to placate the Brahmin priests.

Gwalior to Saugar (Sagar) – 187 miles. This route runs through Jhansi and is acceptable, but not outstanding. You are crossing the Deccan through fine teak forests in hilly country. Saugar used to be the great cavalry centre in British Indian days.

Saugar (Sagar) to Nagpur – 144 miles. The road is similar to the above. Nagpur is a large town, formerly the capital of the Central Provinces. Nagpur oranges are famous all over India. See Chapter 22 for Jabalpur and Pachmarhi which can be approached off this stretch.

Nagpur to Hyderabad – 304 miles. I have not personally used this route from Nagpur to Bangalore, but on paper it appears acceptable. Driving conditions are as above and Hyderabad is a large and interesting city, the capital of Andhra Pradesh.

Hyderabad to Bangalore – 343 miles. Driving conditions as above.

Bangalore to Madras – 206 miles – (National Highway 4). Bangalore is delightful, semi-hill station with all facilities, gracious buildings and parks, from here you descend to the River Palarat Ranipet and then cross an irrigated plain to Madras.

ROUTE 2 – Delhi to Madras via Gwalior, Indore, Poona and Bangalore – 1,603 miles

Although this is longer than route 1, it takes you past many interesting places such as Shivpuri, Mandu, Ellora and Ajanta (see Chapter 22).

Delhi to Gwalior – 197 miles – (National Highways 2 and 3). See above.

Gwalior to Shivpuri – 70 miles – (National Highway 3). The road through Gwalior is narrow and winding, much complicated by the railway. For Shivpuri see Chapter 22. Neither the road nor the driving conditions are outstanding. The country is attractive, being largely scrub jungle.

Shivpuri to Indore – 228 miles – (National Highway 3). Road surfaces vary and one is now climbing up and down the Deccan hills. Indore is a large town with all facilities.

Indore to Dhulia – 162 miles – (National Highway 3). Fifteen miles out of Indore you pass through Mhow, a large military station. Thirteen miles on again you come to Manpur where you can turn right for Mandu (see Chapter 22). The winding road descends to the Narmada River and then crosses the Satpura range. It is particularly difficult between Manpur and Dahivad, ninety-five miles on.

Dhulia to Nasik – 100 miles – (National Highway 3). The road is as before and the countryside of a more open and rolling nature. After a time you go down the Godavari valley and reach Nasik after crossing the river. Here you can continue on to Bombay or strike south to Poona, thus avoiding the huge and congested town. India's most important port, Bombay has grown enormously in the last few years and the people consider that what they think today, India will think tomorrow. It is however subject to riots. Nasik is one of the holy places of India and well worth a stay.

Nasik to Poona – 123 miles – (National Highway 50). The road runs through Sangamner and Manchar and is motorable but not outstanding. At Poona you pick up National Highway 4 from Bombay.

Poona to Belgaum – 210 miles – (National Highway 4). Here you are running across the highly cultivated Deccan plateau.

Belgaum to Bangalore – 307 miles – (National Highway 4). The nature of the road is as before. You are now travelling through Karnataka (Mysore). The country is still quite high and is distinguished by huge lumps of rock that look as if a giant had carelessly dropped them.

Bangalore to Madras – 206 miles – (National Highway 4). See above.

22. *Your Holiday in India and Pakistan*

You will have to plan from the information you get from guide books and tourist pamphlets in following your own particular bent during your holiday. I have written about the actual physical travel to and through the country, but I am not a tourist guide. You may be interested only in wild life or in historical remains. You may want to study the customs of the various peoples and their art, particularly music and dance, so different from our own. You may want to shoot and fish or trek and climb mountains. I can't go with you down these and even more spokes from the hub of Delhi. There are, however, a few broad principles worth considering before you all scatter on your diverse ways.

Your holiday will not be a piece of cake, nor do I think that you wish it to be; you wouldn't plan to come all this way by road, if you were not prepared to take the rough with the smooth. India can be exasperating and it can be lovable. It has yet to learn much about tourism and how to give as well as take. This will be a quite different sort of holiday from any other you'll ever have. It is a vast land with a thousand different peoples, customs and languages, a land of beautiful scenery and flat dullness. There will be moments when you curse the day you came, but all the time you are absorbing rich experience, so that instead of your 'once in a lifetime' visit you will be thinking of another one based on what you have learned. You may go back in some ways disappointed, but you will never shake India off. One day when you are painting a wall or doing something else dull, India will call you, at first faintly and then more loudly. What triggers me off is the cooing of the collared dove, that recent settler from the east.

PLANNING YOUR TRAVELS

When planning your travels in the sub-continent, I would suggest striking a balance between visiting places of historic interest and taking quite a bit of time off to get a breather, so that you can stop and mull over what you have seen and plan for more. There is no better place for this than the Indian jungle. Be it rain, teak or scrub forest, it is for me a fairy land. I take quite a lot of time off in wild life sanctuaries. The places of historic and present day social interest are widely separated by thickly congested, bumpy roads, so that you need a break from time to time. Get the dust off and get your motoring legs back into trim by walking along dappled glades where striped and dappled animals live. Wild Life sanctuaries are organized areas and you will find you will be glad to get away there where you have protection from the millions of pushing, smiling, handsome faces who smother you with friendship and curiosity.

The Central Government Tourist Bureau on the Jan Path, New Delhi, will tell you of the principal wild life parks, though you may have to drag information and pamphlets out of them. Go too to the tourist bureaux of the particular States you intend to visit, to find out about the smaller, less well-known places. These offices are dotted about near Connaught Place. While doing so, find out the few areas where law and order may be temporarily or generally suspect. Dacoits do exist and leaguer up in wild places such as the Thambal Gorges and Shivpuri in central India.

EASTWARDS

Corbett National Wild Life Park and Kaziranga. As you go east from Delhi I would suggest a visit to Corbett Park in Uttar Pradesh. Corbett is only two hundred miles away, through Muradabad on the road to Lucknow. It is a tiger and elephant park, beautiful and well worth the visit in non-monsoon times, and is also emerging as an outstanding bird sanctuary. Kaziranga Park is a much harder and longer drive – so much so that you may well choose to fly in from Calcutta. There you can see the rare Indian rhino as well as tiger.

Corbett is well placed to make a short journey to Rhanikhet to get a serene view of the really big Himalayan peaks. Lansdowne is a little farther, but the view perhaps even better. Mussoorie above Dehra Dun is not that far either, but the view is less good. These places are very cold in winter. You might choose to stop at Corbett Park on your way to Nepal. The recognized route into Nepal is via Muzaffarpur and Raxaul, northeast of Benares (Varanasi), and then on to Kathmandu. Alternatively, you can go on to Lucknow, Benares and Calcutta after your breather in the jungle. I must confess that nowadays, having travelled all over India, I just stay there for the winter!

WESTWARDS

Rajasthan – Siriska. When travelling westwards I would not go as far as Gir, the lion sanctuary. These lions are artificially fed as the scrub forest has dried up through drought and the inroads of grazing cattle. You must, though, visit Rajasthan where the people have the pride of warrior races and dress gaily and well and are handsome. On your way to Jaipur, the great centre of Rajput culture, you can go for a short stay to Siriska in Alwar to see perhaps a tiger and certainly a blue bull or nilgai, an interesting animal which looks like a pony in dark blue, but is a species of antelope. You might see a diminutive four-horned antelope and certainly a big grey deer, the Sambhur.

Chitorgarh. From Jaipur I hope you will go on to Chitorgarh, a vast fort perched on one of the many disconnected Arawali Hills. This and Ranthambhor which is wild life sanctuary and Rajput fortress combined, are musts and yet not always mentioned in the guide books. The former is the place where some of the Rajputs' greatest feats of valour were performed and I would prefer it to any. Here the ceremony of Jauhar in which the inhabitants, facing a hopeless siege, donned their ceremonial robes and sallied forth to fight to the death while their womenfolk burned themselves in the cellars of the fortress, was performed three times in two hundred and fifty years. We once parked for the night on the more ruined side of the fortifications among sand grouse, quail and partridge and could almost hear the challenge of the long-departed sentries on the walls.

Mount Abu. While you are still in Rajasthan, my favourite State for touring, you might consider going up lovely Mount Abu and looking at the Jain marble temple where the stone is so skilfully undercut as to look like transparent alabaster. There is a little wild life sanctuary at its summit where you can park by a small artificial lake, with a gazebo built by the original owner, a Maharajah, for the use of himself, 'Fellow Princes and Special Friends'.

Everywhere on this completely isolated mountain there are old maharajahs' palaces, improbable fairy places now quiet except for one shooting lodge, hung, alas, with photos of so many dead tigers. This is now a hotel where they'll let you park, but I prefer the lake higher up.

SOUTHWARDS

Bharatpur. If you go south from Delhi to Agra and Fatephur Sikhri, you can go on to Bharatpur, the famous bird sanctuary and farther south still, a few miles off the main road, little Dholpur with a few panthers and a beautiful lake with thousands of migrating pinkfoot geese at Christmas time – a lovely place for a short stay.

Shivpuri. As you continue towards Bombay, you pass through Gwalior with its fort and Shivpuri, another sanctuary where you have a chance of seeing a tiger by floodlight. I should not try and stay in the jungle by night as there are probably more dacoits than animals there and the authorities will not let you do it. The Circuit House is the usual place for visitors.

Mandu. Still on your way south, towards Bombay, you come to Indore. Shortly after passing through this town there is a road leading off to the right to Mandu, another 'must'. This is a huge fortified plateau where the tombs and palaces built by Afghan invaders in the thirteenth and fourteenth centuries on top of earlier Hindu structures are being restored by the Archaeological Department with materials similar to those originally used. The best place to stay is in the grounds of the Second Class Resthouse which is prettier and farther out of the little bazaar than the First Class one. Here you can learn about the romantic Baz Bahadur, the ballad king and his love, Rupmati, the singer from the sacred Narmada River below.

Ajanta and Ellora. From Mandu you can go on south through Nasik and Poona towards Mysore and on the way you can visit Ajanta and Ellora. The mural paintings at Ajanta show you more of the ancient and varied races of the sub-continent than any statuary. The caves were lived in from the second century BC up to the seventh century AD by Buddhist monks who carved the walls and painted the frescoes. After that they were forgotten until they were rediscovered by a party of Englishmen out shooting in the late nineteenth century. There are Resthouses at both places to shelter you.

The Nilgiris and Periyar Park. There are wild life sanctuaries in the State of Karnataka (Mysore) at Bandipur and Mudamalai. The road from the latter leads to the Nilgiris which are forested hill resorts with rolling downs as well. Farther still is the Periyar Park, favourite for elephants and gaur (wild oxen, *not* bison). These can best be seen from boats along the park's waterways. The south of India abounds with temples and places of historic interest, so you should take your pick from the guide books.

Jabalpur. Another possibility is to turn south-east from Gwalior through Jhansi and the lovely teak forests of central India, which are ideal for camping in undisturbed by crowds, down to Jabalpur which is interesting in itself because of the Marble Rocks, the setting for Mowgli's leap in the *Jungle Book*. The 'Little People' have been destroyed since my childhood, nearly sixty years ago. My father started the first Independent Brigade there and his name persists. From Jabalpur, if you are interested in anthropology you can arrange visits to see the Ghonds, little black people, once the rulers of the land. Their forts are still there. They are drop-outs now and have been thrust into the jungle by northern invaders. They dream their days away, drinking strong liquor distilled from the lovely, waxy golden Mohur blossoms.

Pachmarhi. Jabalpur is a good jumping-off place southwestwards across the Narmada River (it runs straight across India from east to west) to Pachmarhi, the plateau of the Satpuras which you should not miss if you like haunting beauty. It has strangely shaped hills, gorges and waterfalls. There are lovely little corners off the wooded roads where you can camp. You must take an easy day's walk up Dhup Garh Hill and back or stay the night at the bungalow at the top. The name means The House of the Sun and the sun does set between its twin humps. From there you can see tumbled hills for miles and miles which still harbour the gaur and are still wild and unspoilt. Whisps of smoke show the camps of the aboriginals, collectively and vaguely called Ardivasi. You walk through clouds of butterflies among the rocks which are sandstone, weathered black, but red where newly scored. There is a cave at one end of the plateau with as yet unidentified drawings, like bushmen's work, showing hunting scenes and religious ceremonies which seem centred round a sort of Maltese cross, perhaps a stylized sun. The drawings may be quite recent or even very old – no one of course knows, but the cave is very dry, small and well concealed. Ask Puran Singh, a self-appointed guide in Pachmarhi's tiny bazaar to show you the cave. I doubt if many others know it.

Kanha Wild Life Park. From Pachmarhi you can go eastwards to the Kanha Sanctuary, famous for gaur, swamp deer and a few of the remaining handful of the most beautiful and swift antelope in the world – the Black Buck. As a child on a train journey through flat India I remember them in thousands everywhere. Jeeps and spotlights have put an end to that in the last twenty-five years. At the right time of year, that is in the autumn and in February, you can quite easily watch a tiger from a concrete tower as it comes in to kill a bait. Other sanctuaries tend to be a bit scornful and talk about cookhouse pussy cats, but you do at least see the animal in its brilliantly coloured wild state.

Khajuraho. I am always sceptical about glowing tourist guide books and think twice before going to see popular places, but Khajuraho *is* worth seeing, not so much for erotic reasons as for the lay-out and style of the temple buildings. The whole area is peaceful and one is not pestered by guides and beggars. The Chandellas must have been gay and light-hearted, but some would say that at times their gaiety was almost irresponsible. The expression 'indecent' does not spring to mind as one looks at the frank carvings – one gains an impression more of the happy pursuit of creation.

There is a nice place to camp under an umbrella-like tree below the dam of a delightful lake – not the tree with a flag sticking out of the top which is sacred, but the other one. The turn off for this is a few miles short of Khajuraho and is signed.

Konarak. From Khajuraho you can go to Rewa, the original home of the white tigers, or south again and eastwards towards Orissa with the Sun Temple of Konarak near Bhubaneswar, the great centre of temples, and the attractions of bathing at Puri. It is a long way and this area might be better approached from Calcutta. Konarak is as splendid as Khajuraho and one can live down by the beach; be careful of bathing – there are certainly sharks and I think poisonous sea serpents. We saw a magnificent pair of white-bellied sea eagles there once and they live on them.

NORTHWARDS

Kashmir. Kashmir is one of the great beauty spots of the world though somewhat less so than when I used to visit it on leave as a young officer because of deforestation caused by the great increase of population. As I said in an earlier chapter, go there in the summer, not the winter. Try and spend a few days on a houseboat for the experience, if possible in Nagin or Nasim Baghs which are still unspoilt. Avoid the Dal Lake like the plague – it is an aquatic slum – and see that your washing-up is done in clean water, not merely dipped in the lake.

So many campers go up at the wrong time of year. They cannot believe Kashmir, so beautiful with its flowers in the tourist pamphlets, is bitterly cold in the winter, wet and grim in early spring and depressing after the end of November. From late April till the end of October its beauties are not overrated.

A lot of tourists go to shop in Kashmir and the Kashmiris are amongst the most artistically gifted people in the world. Their sense of colour and line is infallible in a world that is becoming increasingly vulgar. If you can, go to the little workshops where they make papier maché, the wood carving, the embroideries and the carpets you see in the shops. Their knotted carpets can match those of Iran, but don't carry such a big price tag.

The best take-off for Kashmir is at Jullundur (p. 153) and the road goes through Pathankot and Jammu up the lofty Bannihal through a tunnel, no longer over the pass, down into the Vale of Kashmir to the capital, Srinagar which has the air more of Central Asia or Iran, than India or Pakistan.

TOURING IN PAKISTAN

I have given the question of touring in Pakistan much thought, and I have a feeling of special responsibility to travellers in this area because of the special opportunities that I have had, to get know it, fighting on its borders between the Wars, living all over the area for years and walking on my flatters in temperatures up to 125° in the shade. I have revisited Pakistan many times since to bring myself up to date and to meet its delightful people.

The Pakistan Tourist Development Corporation which has branches in the principal towns is new and enthusiastic. I feel it probably suffers from growing pains and being ebullient, tends to add too much cochineal to the pink icing. For example, Pakistan does not abound in game, large or small. It was not protected in British times and the numbers of sportsmen have greatly increased since then. The Pakistani is inordinately fond of shooting and the game has but to twitch a whisker to invite a fusillade of shots. People are not protection minded and, alas, the game has been unable to wait till they are.

There is fishing in Swat (see p. 148) and Kaghan, on the Kabul River near Attock, and in the Jhelum. Artificially introduced trout make this form of fishing available in Swat and Kaghan and the mahseer, that mighty game fish, moves up the small rivers from the Indus when the water warms. Unfortunately the Tarbela and Mangla dams are severely restricting passage now and the mahseer no longer gets up to Kashmir for example. Trout fishing is best in late summer as snow water spoils it earlier.

You can motor up to Kaghan by the Abbottabad route and enjoy the scenery and fishing. If you wish to go farther into the valley than Naran some 40 m. beyond Kaghan you would probably have to hire a jeep, particularly if you wish to visit Hunza. I personally am most reluctant to leave my camper, my home and citadel, in anyone's charge for long at a time. In the east, at the best it will be climbed over by innumerable children and scratched – orientals however hospitable are over-indulgent parents. The mirrors will come off having been twisted by the local bucks admiring themselves and curling their moustaches.

If you do wish to fly to Chitral, Gilgit or Hunza it is expensive, but rewarding. If you engage the services of the Tourist Development Corporation for any such trip, your expenses will naturally mount and you must be prepared for this. Permits will almost certainly be required for the latter two places and obtaining them through the Tourist bureaus may take a long time.

As the well-known tourist attractions are few and very far between, these are best done should your route pass nearby. For example, if you want to see Mohenjo Daro or Harappa, I do not advise the ordinary traveller to make a special trip. If you are travelling from Lahore to Quetta, turn off and visit them on the way (see Chapter 24). You and I, though reverent before these relics of some of the earliest cities, will soon tire of looking at foundations and want to move on after an hour or two. In the same way Taxila can be visited when travelling along the other main route (Peshawar to Lahore) – see Chapter 20.

Pakistan is on the north-west side of the sub-continent and therefore the climate tends to be extreme. In principle do not tour the predominantly low country in summer as it will be unpleasantly hot – hotter than southern India. Do not visit the mountain resorts in winter. It will be freezing. So in between your visits to mountain resorts in summer, scuttle as quickly as a scorpion across the hot plains. In Peshawar and Rawalpindi you need a fire round the clock in January and December and Lahore is not much warmer, or even Delhi across the border. Thus you will see how important my remarks are in Chapter 7 suggesting that your camper be heavily insulated from heat and cold.

THE COMMISSARIAT

When you are travelling you can buy food from roadside kitchens. Be careful and buy curry and rice, etc. piping hot and put it into your own containers. Spices can conceal bad meat so it is often better to be a vegetarian. Prathas cooked before you are delicious, so are chapattis and a few scalding ladlefuls of dhal (lentils). Bread is replaced by rather insipid rice cakes call Idlies in the nether half of India.

Choose food stalls/kitchens well out of fly-blown, dusty towns and above all go to the ones the truck drivers patronize. They know good food, especially the Sikhs. These kitchens have to be on open ground outside the villages to allow room for the trucks to park, so all in all it will be a cleaner, fresher area. You may find yourself in lively conversation with a bearded Sikh driver, friendly and extrovert, as you sit together on a string bed set out in the shade.

23. *Indian Hospitality*

You are not likely to have been more than a few hours in the country before some pleasant stranger will invite you to stay with him and his family. I think you should be a little careful of such invitations and try and find out a bit about where you are going. If your new friend lives on his farm, deep in the country, look out. You may impose enormous strain on your precious vehicle to reach this farm through deep sand, mud or rivers.

Life in India is generally rather dull for the inhabitants who do not fill in their time to quite the same extent as we do in the west. A life that seems strange and romantic to us is just old hat and boring to the people who actually live it. It would be undignified for an Indian gentleman to do his own house or car repairs, dig or plant his garden or have other manual hobbies. Books are now more readily available, but the habit of reading is not widespread. A game of cards is popular, but best of all is a good chat in the sun for hours at a time, generally about money. You are new people from a strange country and there is much to enquire about and neighbours will be called in. Your host is then a social success and you are a prized exhibit. Do not feel you are a sort of performing curiosity – but you are of course. Don't let it irk you, especially if you are young and resilient. After all you have come to see and meet nice people.

A VISIT TO THE COUNTRY

I was once asked to visit a distinguished landowner deep in the country. I had, he felt, tried to do a good turn for his son serving in the forces and he wished to show his gratitude. He also wished to meet an Englishman, for many of his honours dated from the time of the British. He was thirsty for knowledge of the outside world and for fresh ideas, as his political activities were perhaps beginning to pall in a new and rapidly changing world, where ripples were already making his possession of considerable lands less assured. I'm sorry to say the splendid old man, as indeed he was, was murdered by a political enemy soon after I last visited him.

I asked the son about the journey from New Delhi out to his father's farm, as I had an idea that the going would be hard. I was assured that the road would be excellent all the way. I was greatly tempted to go as in my latter days I have tried to get closer to the people I like so much and to get away from the military cantonment life of my youth. Camping has opened up a more intimate contact with the real, colourful India.

So we set off to meet his father. I was quite firm in refusing to take a number of passengers who suddenly materialized. In India, no sooner is a rubber tyre about to roll, than people pile into a vehicle as a matter of course. Thank God, I was firm! As we got deeper into the country, the road got worse and worse. I had a through cab then and we sucked foul dust into the back which was vibrating so much that the fittings were just a fuzzy haze. The road became a sandy track, lined with grasping thorn bushes to score my paint, and then we dipped into a river, sticking and churning across, consoled and reassured by my passenger now squatting on the seat with his feet well out of the wash. I was by now extremely querulous and reproached him and abused all and everything in a mannerless way. I was told we had only a mile or so to go. Easterns in their kindly hearts always tell you that which they hope will please you. The grim reality was yet to unfold. There was more deep sand, mud and a broader river. What price hub grease seals, what price an engine desperately over-revved to avoid foundering in a rapidly developing quicksand overlaid by a whirlpool?

At last we arrived. Our host was a magnificent and powerfully built figure with a strong, hooked nose and sweeping white moustaches. He had the peculiarly full eye of a well-bred Indian with much white showing below the irises. I took to him at once. We, that is my wife and I and he chatted for hours and ate highly spiced fish from his river and drank Scotch whisky which costs a maharajah's ransome in India. It was very pleasant except for the fact that our chat was largely a monologue by our host, for Indians never listen. I like monologues too, but I met my match.

Then came the question of settling in for the night. Our host was head of a considerable village, peopled by relations and retainers in the centre of his lands. We were ushered into a cell-like hut. We asked about toilet facilities but this in India is an unembarrassing minor problem. A walled enclosure two feet high was indicated with a plain mud floor and nothing else. This was down by the main path through the village. As it was looked down on and into by every building there, it was simply not on. As discomfort increased, we cast glances this way and that with ever more anxious eyes. At last I realized that the only course was to make some excuse to get something out of our camper – in those days a dormobile with no 'facilities' – which was in a yard with a bit of straw about and huge domestic buffaloes. We ducked down behind the caravan in turn, the other keeping a lookout.

The cell had hard beds and was sited at the foot of a large pepul tree. We went to bed tired with the strain of the journey and of maintaining pleasantries hour after hour in a foreign language, however familiar. Then as we dozed and drifted into sleep the pepul tree city woke up to begin the night. As is the nature of these trees it was full of small animals, reptiles, bats and anything else that crawled, hopped or slithered. Having slept on bare ground in the open for many months on active service I was hardened to discomfort. It was not so for my wife. The bustle and hustle in and around the tree became more and more active and was equally uncomfortable for us both. First, dust and grit fell on our faces as things crawled along the rough ceiling beams. Then I changed my position and my hard pillow buzzed like one of those trick buzzers which you palm before shaking hands. As you shake, it vibrates and your victim whips his hand away as you all fall down in paroxysms of jolly laughter. Something was being squashed under my pillow. I shifted and there was a plop on the floor. As mutterings, faint squeaks and chirrups went on over an undertone of slithering and pattering, our heated and tired imaginations took flight. The Pepul People had come to investigate us. We dared not move for fear of putting out a hand on a cobra's hood or a scorpion's arched tail.

Even this night came to an end, and pale and weary, we had a good breakfast and went on a partridge shoot. But where to go for the increasing demands of nature? We looked at a solitary buffalo. Would it provide sufficient cover in the flat, reaped, winter landscape, or would it move at the critical moment? At last we found a screening hedgerow and abruptly broke away from the party. They, as is usual in the Indian countryside, had gone out to the hedgerows near the village before dawn, carrying little brass 'lotahs' of water.

Early on, we had seen that the future was bleak, so I developed and enlarged upon a pressing engagement we had to fulfil and we parted that afternoon with no skin off any nose.

It had been a grey day when we arrived, so I expressed anxiety about rain possibly filling the rivers we had crossed to cut us off. Oh no, it never rained at this time of year we were assured. It did and briskly. The retreat was cut. It's all right, they said, you can get out along this lane and they described a detour of many miles. We set out with a guide. The lane soon resembled Passchendaele. We revved mightily and churned forward inch by inch, often swinging sideways on, twirling the wheel backwards and forwards for hours until we reached a tarmac road of sorts. The camper was never the same again, its gallant heart had been strained.

The next year when we came out with a new and better-appointed camper of my own design. I declared flatly that we'd accept no more invitations. I called on my regiment as usual. This was a fatal step. I was met by the son, a fine upstanding young officer who said, 'You must come to my wedding,' his handsome eyes glowing softly with hospitality. 'My father is looking forward so much. It will mean so much to have a British officer from the old days, etc., etc.'

AN INDIAN WEDDING

I gave way. Was it that a year, only a year, had dimmed the horrific memories? Or was I just plain soft? I agreed, but as a good soldier hastily drew up a plan of operation. I said that all would agree that the last bit of the road was a bit tough, even by the shortest route and anyway there'd be a lot of guests and accommodation would be tight. (By then I was desperately snatching new defences out of the air: The mind was simply racing.) I said I would stop on the bank of the first river and would he arrange for someone at that little tea shop there to keep an eye on the vehicle? Then would he send his riding ponies so that we could do the last bit mounted? In any case, the worst bit was only seven miles and two rivers to cross. All was agreed and we would come.

I was fully aware of the honour of being invited to see a high class Hindu wedding, as they are exclusive affairs. I'd only seen one once before when the Rajah of Bobbili, near Vizianagram, invited me to his daughter's wedding many years ago and even then I only had a distant view from a crenellated wall of the palace.

We set off once more to our doom and as tactfully as possible fended off a belated surge of retainers hoping to bow our springs. We were to

meet a gallant Colonel, friend of the family, en route and travel together.
He failed to turn up at the rendezvous for hours. When he did he said
he'd had nine punctures. I believe it. Tyres were then very scarce and his
showed the canvas. He complained that his son, a rather fat poached egg,
had let the car run dry of engine oil too and he'd had to fill up. It was
certainly a very sick car. His pudgy son wagged his head as only an
Indian can and said, 'Doubtless you can put in double quantity w'oil
next time, Daddy!'

We arrived at an outlying village on the estate – our next rendezvous –
where the previous year we had been met and conducted on. We waited
another hour and then a small boy whom we'd noticed asleep, woke up.
He handed us a note of polite greeting which said that my host had gone
on. We were certainly late, due to the Colonel who had finally come to
rest in a cloud of evil smelling smoke. We had pretended not to notice
this and left him to his fate.

We went on in trepidation to our particular Styx and waited a long
time on its banks by the teashop. At last a tractor came across with some
brothers of the bridegroom-to-be. They had a puncture in the
front wheel. Had we a pump? Of course I had. I have lent that poor
footpump to thousands of improvident Indians far nearer base than I
was. We pumped madly in turns, each doing 'our purple', but gained
little on the leak.

I mentioned the ponies and the watchman. 'Oh, father says you can't
possibly stay out in the jungle. What would the neighbours say! An
honoured guest was not entertained under his roof, they would say.'

Did I mutter, 'And under that damned pepul tree'? So I put our new
camper's nose down into Father Styx and after an hour's desperate
struggle reached our haven of despair.

I greeted my host in the rather effusive embrace which is the custom in
the east. You see the Russians doing it to their astronauts. We all settled
down to a good talk but I could not find out the programme for the
next day. In the morning, after breakfast they said. 'We're off.'

'Off where?' I asked.

'Oh, to Jammu for the wedding, only two hundred miles.'

I knew that bride and groom visited both families for the induction
ceremonies, but had had the impression that the wedding was to be in
the village. I decided to go to Jammu in the camper rather than in the
family bus. I was not going to be separated from my home. It was

agreed that we would meet for a late lunch at the Jammu Tourist Resthouse.

We arrived at this shabby pile and waited hours while urchins pestered us. Late in the afternoon the eldest son and organizer arrived and said, 'Oh, there you are. We missed you at lunch at so and so and wondered what had happened to you. Come over to the Circuit House. We are all staying there.' All this was news to us.

Eventually, leaving our vehicle at the Circuit House we were driven up to the wedding in the procession with the Chief of Police. The streets were a seething mass as it was the season for weddings and the pundits had all chosen the same propitious days. There were strings of coolies with double petromax lamps on their heads threading through other strings of coolies with petromaxes on their heads. All was lights, bobbing away as they wove their way to weddings and from weddings in that characteristic bent-knee amble of the Indian human beast of burden. Weddings are handed over to contractors who do everything from pretty rain effects in coloured lights to shamianas (marquees), to food and to the bridegroom's steed. Doing a cut-price job, one lay-out would be packed up to be set up again at another wedding at the other end of the town and already desperately late. The bridegroom's charger which had to be white had long left the shafts and found all this dashing about exhausting. Its tinselly finery, saddle cloth and great plume did not conceal the fact that it was ill cast for the present happy role and better fitted to carry the figure of famine in the Apocalyptic four. Dingy white horses with nodding plumes stumbled past each other and criss-crossed in narrow streets, making a pattern with the petrol lamps, rolled shamianas and other nuptial finery, late, lost and muddled.

When we arrived I was introduced to the bride's father and party as the Brigadier who had come ten thousand miles to the wedding. The home side fell silent. They had nothing to put in to bat against this.

The ceremony was about to start and the son, a fine figure, gay in a long, high collared coat of pale gold brocade and a bright turban with a jewelled egret feather, looked magnificent. His curved sword was at his side. His turban tied in the Rajput mode, had great style as it came down low on one side in tight rolls with a dashing air. But wait a minute! Oh, his charger – poor brute, its head hung to the ground. In India the drop from the sublime to tragi-comic is steep and sudden.

There was a ceremonial introduction of the groom by his father and sponsors to the males of the bride's family with a token wrestling match between the two fathers – a relic of the past when the bride was seized and carried away. This was all pure ceremony for the two families were great friends.

I wanted to see the whole ceremony and record it in my mind clearly, but I was joined by a stout elderly individual. He wore a sort of fore and aft Gandhi cap of ginger cat's skin which had seen bad times in life and after. He wore too a black, formal atchkan, but something had gone wrong with the neck fastenings of the high collar and a bright blue and white striped pyjama collar had escaped from beneath and lodged behind his ear. He definitely lacked style. Apparently he loved the British, so we had something in common. A good start, but what about the finish? My new friend would, I hoped, tell me about the inner meaning of the elaborate and attractive Hindu marriage ceremony. I started to ask questions, but was overwhelmed with declarations of love for the British. I became feverishly restive in my efforts to break away from this diatribe. In my imagination bromide followed cliché in a sort of ephemeral dance, rising up on a thermal from his heated brain. He emphasized his ill-informed but laudatory remarks about the old British Raj with sharp taps upon my forearm. He admired Churchill, so did I. He said what a wonderful, selfless man he was to step aside and let socialism have a chance in the election immediately after World War II. I doubted if Churchill had seen it like that, but no longer had the physical energy to argue.

I did see something of the wedding, but it was hard to follow in its intricate ceremonial, due to the bombardment on my flank. I was, however, struck by its great charm. The bride and groom were seated in a little golden bower of slender framework adorned with tinsel and marigolds. She wore a brilliant flame coloured sari with a foot-deep border of gold thread – this real gold never tarnishes. Her face was concealed by a fringe of gold hanging from the sari drawn over her head. It made me think of a gay bird with jewelled eyes in a golden cage – a confection by Fabergé.

The pundit or priest directed the ceremony, intoning endlessly in Sanskrit. He wore a threadbare brown pillbox on his head and had slung a long, dirty white woollen scarf rakishly round his neck and down his back like a rowing blue. His coat was well worn as were his bare feet and legs which emerged from that least attractive of all male nether garments, the wrap round, hitch and no stitch dhoti. I looked at the deep cracks in the soles of his feet and his tired slippers beside them. His acolyte was a half-starved wraith of still greater shabbiness. Holiness was obviously not very profitable in these parts, for he was a well-known and much revered man.

At one point the bride fed the groom from bright brass bowls full of coloured food on a brass tray. What a picture! Her hands were light golden and her fingers long. The well-to-do young Indian woman does not use her hands for heavy work, unlike her western counterpart, and so her hands feel boneless and the fingers bend backwards pliantly. This giving of food was done with grace and shortly preceded the culminating ceremony when the pundit fastened the clothes of bride and groom together as they rose to circle round the fire in the centre of the cage. The flames picked up the glitter of the gold sari border and the girl's nostril jewels. Then there was a pause. The parents had now joined the couple in the birdcage, and all were looking a bit embarrassed. The bride's father was to wash the groom's feet. There was no hot water – no water at all. Raucous shouts rent the air for the bhisti or water carrier of the house. There was much clanking behind the scenes.

The guests had been wandering about, the women glittering with jewels, their golden-skinned midriffs catching the light. But their voices were loud and often strident and drowned the pundit's droning. There was no reverence. Was it because in the east a marriage is primarily a business contract? 'Oh my dear, we did things quite differently at *my* daughter's wedding, etc, etc.' Some wives even tapped the nearest person in the birdcage and offered loud advice.

The bhisti clattered back on bowed matchstick legs with a galvanized bucket of warm water for the washing ceremony. He plunked it down in the middle of the cage, salaamed and drew back into the dark. The washing proceeded. 'Oh, a towel! Where's the towel? Who's pinched that d . . .' Loud shouts for a towel and after a while a servant trotted up with a hand towel with a large curry stain on it.

Am I being unkind? Possibly, but I was by then sorely tried by my neighbour. Of course it was really a lovely ceremony with exquisitely beautiful moments. One tends to forget that religion is a rather matey affair in the east, domestic rather than ecclesiastical.

We bumped back next day to the village, or rather we elected to camp hidden deep in the trees on the river bank. The wedding bus wheezed past late at night and stuck fast in river number two. We joined the party at the village tactfully late next morning as we had heard the bus's churnings in the river till the small hours.

That day there was a partridge shoot. The Colonel had at last arrived and every time I shot a partridge shouted loudly, 'Oh my God, the Brigadier has shot a bird;' in a congratulatory sort of way. The party was not taking them well on the wing otherwise.

On our return there was a dance cum concert. In the unsophisticated rural districts it is more proper for dancing 'girls' to be males. I think it downright obscene. These painted males in saris and ankle bells circled carefully in the centre of the ring of seated guests. All except we westerners were able to sit cross-legged for hours. The entertainers sang in high, cracked voices, breaking off suddenly to step over legs and take a proffered coin. This would be followed by a special bit of singing in praise of the donor. The singing was varied by slapstick comedy in which a pig's bladder belaboured the funny man unmercifully. We might have been in the Middle Ages and certainly the festivity seemed to last as long.

Our parts as guests fully played, we left with many invitations for the future. It had been most interesting and looking back now that the aches and pains have gone, I would not have missed it. It's only that our ways are so different. Theirs was the charm and theirs the generosity.

24. *The Ribs and the Limbs –*
Pakistan and Iran

DISTANCES AND TIMES

Lahore to Multan	..	..	..	220 miles	1 day
Multan to Sukkur	..	..	..	275 miles	1 day
Sukkur to Quetta	..	..	..	255 miles	1 day
Quetta to Kandahar (Afghanistan)	..			149 miles	6 hours
Quetta to Zahedan (Iran)	..		..	448 miles	

(This will take at least two days, possibly more. The 85 miles of No Man's Land between the Pakistan and Iranian customs posts takes over 5 hours alone.)

Zahedan to Kerman	..	..	..	336 miles	

(The first 130 miles could take you a day and you might be held up by a flooded river. Thereafter you can count on an average speed of of 40 m.p.h.)

Kerman to Isfahan	..	..	..	440 miles	11 hours plus
Isfahan to Teheran	..	..	..	278 miles	7 hours
Isfahan to Persepolis	..	..	..	273 miles	7 hours
Persepolis to Shiraz	..	..	..	35 miles	1 hour
Mashhad to Teheran (via the road South of the Elburz)	..	..	..	511 miles	2½ days

If you have time on your way home from India you can vary your route and even visit places that are well off it – the ribs and limbs of your Backbone. You have after all achieved your major objective and can perhaps give yourself an extra treat on the way back.

PAKISTAN – THE ROAD TO QUETTA

The first variant possible is to strike west at Lahore and return through Quetta, the capital of Baluchistan. This road leaves much to be desired and whatever you do, don't believe the maps which show several alternative routes. There is only one that is feasible – that from Lahore through Multan, the Sukkur Barrage and Jacobabad. We did this eight years ago and vowed never to do it again as the road was so bad between Multan and Jacobabad. It is better now and travellers are doing it successfully.

On your way home, coming to Lahore from the Wagah-Attari border, go up the Mall as far as the Telecommunication Centre and there turn left. The road to Multan is straightforward and signed all the way.

Lahore to Multan – 220 miles. In Multan almost the only place to stop is in the grounds of the Canal Resthouse – rather hot and noisy even in late February. At Sahiwal, 105 m. from Lahore you can turn off for Harappa (see Chapter 22).

Multan to Sukkur – 275 miles. Sukkur is the next reasonable stopping place for the night and one can usually camp in the garden of the Engineers' Rest-house above the Barrage, which you cross to proceed to Quetta.

Sukkur to Quetta – 255 miles. Twenty-five miles out is the turning for Mohenjo Daro (see Chapter 22) 55 miles S.W. You later pass Jacobabad, one of the hottest places in the sub-continent. There is one pass before Quetta – the Bolan at 5,900 ft. After this you climb again to Quetta at 6,500 ft. If you then plan to go home through Afghanistan you can get your visa at the Afghan Trade Mission.

Quetta to Kandahar – 149 miles. The road is narrow and mountainous in places. The Afghan border is at Spin Baldak, some eighty-five miles from Quetta and at Kandahar you are back on your original route.

IRAN

Quetta to Zahedan – 448 miles. Think very carefully before you decide to take the route through southern Iran via Zahedan. Although you avoid snow in early spring, the road is very bad in places and there is always the danger of flooding. The scrape parts of the road are particularly bad and we broke a Land-Rover spring there. It had not improved last winter and people were driving along in the desert rather than on the road.

From Quetta the road goes through the Baluchistan desert to the border and Zahedan fifty miles beyond it. It is lonely with little traffic and the surface fair to appalling. Do not stop or be stopped for anyone as this whole area is insecure. There is petrol at Nushki at ninety-three miles and at Nok Kundi, the Pakistan Customs (350 miles out), height 5,600 ft. These are the places to spend the night if you cannot get through to Iran in a day. Once in Iran you can camp wild.

The next petrol is at Mirjawa (Mirdjaveh), on the Iranian border, lovely cheap Iranian petrol. From Mirjawa to Zahedan (50 m) the road is rough and corrugated.

Zahedan to Kerman – 336 miles. Zahedan is a good night stop and you should fill up all tanks as the next petrol is at Bam – two hundred and ten slow miles. The first hundred and thirty miles are bad and corrugated and then the road is cut by a river that has no bridge and frequently floods. The flood can be a mile wide. There is a caterpillar tractor on the farther bank to tow you across.

From here onwards the road is good tarmac except for a half mile stretch, four miles east of Bam, which is at 4,200 ft and a few bad bits between Bam and Kerman. On the other side of Bam there is one easy pass of 8,700 ft. Kerman lies at 6,300 ft at the intersection of this highway from Pakistan and the principal caravan routes across the desert. Kerman produced some of the most beautiful carpets of Iran. Originally the inhabitants specialized in 'Paisley Shawls' and when these became unfashionable in the west, they turned to the manufacture of carpets, using many of the fine designs from the shawls.

Kerman to Isfahan – 440 miles. The desert is always beautiful and made still more exciting by the play of light and shade as the day advances. In Iran there always seem to be splendid mountains on the horizon and on this journey you pass through them several times. Yezd (Yazd) is two hundred and thirty-five miles from Kerman and is a quite large town with mechanics. The great gateway of the Masjid-i-Jomeh is its most notable ornament. Naiñ, another hundred and fifteen miles on is another carpet centre whose products are much prized by collectors. There is one more easy pass before Isfahan, at 8,200 ft.

Isfahan to Teheran – 278 miles. The best route is by Saveh. It is quite straightforward and is tarmac all the way, though the tar often suffers from winter frost. In February the road can be blocked by snow.

Isfahan. If you have not come to Isfahan from the east on your way home, you simply must make a side trip from Teheran, preferably in April when the city which lies at 5,500 ft will be at its best. (See Chapter 18 for exit from Teheran.)

I will touch on its beauties, but do read up about it before you visit it. It was chosen as his capital by Shah Abbas in the sixteenth century and became the centre of a brilliant empire and culture. This period saw the development of the art of carpet weaving in its highest classical form and the emperor encouraged the work of both craftsmen and designers.

In modern times Reza Shah ordered a restoration of the wonderful buildings of those earlier times that had been left so long to moulder.

The Royal Square is huge – some say comparable in size to the Red Square in Moscow. It was a polo ground whose stone goal posts still stand. It is circled by low buildings fronted by a double tier of brick arches. The Ali Kapu, or Exalted Gate, on one side was part grandstand and part gateway to the royal palaces, now mostly gone, though the Pavilion of Forty Pillars (Chehel Situn) with its paintings of court life still exists.

Opposite to it is the café-au-lait coloured dome of the Sheikh Lutfullah Mosque, in unusual contrast to the other blue domes. The mosque is unusual in another way – it is covered in, with no customary open square for worshippers, being built for the ladies of the royal entourage.

The Royal Mosque, dating from the sixteenth century is off-set at an angle to the square in order to face towards Mecca. When a service is not in progress it gives a feeling of great peace.

Leading off the opposite end of the square is the covered bazaar. There carpets are thrown down for camels and handcarts to pass over in an effort to hasten their antiquity.

The Madrasseh-i-Madar-i-Shah (Ecclesiastical College) lies on the Chahar Bagh Avenue. My wife and I have actually looked down from the balcony of one of its minarets. The custodian was so delighted when I pretended to understand that he had fifty children that he let us go up provided the mullah did not see us.

Isfahan to Persepolis – 273 miles. If you can afford the time turn then southwards to Persepolis, the Achaemenid capital. There is a good road all the way. Shortly before Persepolis you will see the turning to the right for Naqsh-i-Rustum, the modern name for the Valley of the Kings, where Darius I and many of his successors were buried in rock tombs, cut into the wall of the valley. Below them is a splendid series of wall carvings showing the battles between the Sassanid king, Shapur and the Romans, with the Emperor Valerian kneeling before the king in abject submission.

Persepolis looks just as you would expect – slightly vulgar Hollywood epic. Elizabeth Taylor would just suit the place, serpenting round the columns of the Apadana. Still, it has majesty and is impressive in the evening glow of the sunset. You can see a nilgai in the procession of gifts to Darius in the great bas-relief below the staircase of the Apadana, for northern India was in his empire.

Persepolis to Shiraz – 35 miles. Shiraz is a city of gardens and noted as the home and burial place of Saadi and Hafiz – Iran's two greatest poets. Having got as far as this, you would be wise to return through Isfahan. The roads to the Gulf are rough and narrow and night driving is prohibited since they cross the territory of the Kashgai tribe who still lead a nomadic life and might resent intruders.

Mashhad to Teheran, south of the Elburz – 511 miles. If it is your object to avoid snow on the Elburz passes on your way west, you can travel south of the Elburz round the Dash-e-Kever (Salt Desert). The road is rough and corrugated after Neishabur where the tarmac gives out eighty-five miles from Mashhad, but it is warm all the way. From Neishabur you go through Shahrud, Damghan, Semnan and Sharifabad to Teheran. Avoid the Bashm pass through which the motoring organizations route you. It is rightly named.

25. The Ribs and the Limbs – Turkey

DISTANCES AND TIMES		
The Black Sea, Erzerum to Trabzon ..	204 miles	1 day
Trabzon to Samsun	227 miles	1 day
Samsun to Ankara	266 miles	1 day
Ankara to Göreme and Urgup	259 miles	1 day
Sivas to Göreme and Urgup	119 miles	6 hours
The South Coast and Aegean, Ankara to Tarsus	285 miles	1 day
Tarsus to Korikos	55 miles	
Korikos to Antalya	270 miles	1 day
Antalya to Dinar	113 miles	4 hours
Dinar to Seljuk (Akincilar)	172 miles	5 hours
Seljuk (Akincilar) to Canakkale	242 miles	1 day
Ecebat to Keşan	75 miles	3 hours
Canakkale to Bursa	193 miles	5 hours
Izmir to Bursa	220 miles	1 day
Ankara to Bursa	242 miles	1 day
Bursa to Istamboul	152 miles	5 hours

When you come to Turkey there are so many alternative routes that I feel it should be done on its own, since the best weather can be in early and late summer. The spring can be cold and wet. The main alternative route to that by which you came is conveniently described as the Black Sea route.

THE BLACK SEA

Erzerum to Trabzon – 204 miles. If you return this way, follow the original road Westwards out of Erzerum as far as Askale and there at the petrol station bear right for the Kondagi Gecidi, eighteen miles away, height 7,840 ft. There is no tarmac after eight miles and the road

is steep with a lot of hairpins. The whole way to the sea is narrow with a
bad surface and unfriendly inhabitants. There are two more passes
before Trabzon – the Vuvak Gecidi, 6,266 ft and the Zigana Pass,
6,600 ft. The latter is very long, climbing from Torul at 3,100 ft and
dropping to Trabzon at sea level. In spring the flowers are wonderful,
particularly the primroses.

Trabzon to Samsun – 227 miles. The road runs along the coast and
there are plenty of places to stop. Beware all the time of mad truck
drivers. They are particularly reckless in this district. The hazel nut
plantations are probably the best in the world and it was the rhodo-
dendron honey of Trabzon that drove Xenophon's men out of their
senses. The road is fair tarmac, but there are some bad stretches of
potholes. It hugs the sea on the whole, except between Esbiye and
Kesap, sixty-five and eighty-five miles respectively out of Trebzon,
where it winds over a low pass.

Samsun to Ankara – 266 miles. Samsun is a large seaport, but the road
to Ankara skirts round it on the sea flank. Just beyond the town the road
turns left up into the hills and shortly passes two petrol stations where
one can spend the night. The road is up and down as always in Turkey
and not very good. It rejoins the original road at Cerikli, a hundred and
eighty-seven miles out from Samsun.

GÖREME AND URGUP

There is a series of monasteries and chapels, carved out of the grey
cone-like knolls of pumice stone that cover the area at the former and
an immense underground city near the latter. The effect is very ghostly.
I keep thinking I see some Brueghel-like figures out of the corner of my
eye, shuffling and dragging themselves behind a cone. Persecuted
Christians had to hide somewhere. You get there from Kayseri, fifty-
five miles away which can be approached either from Ankara (204 m) or
Sivas (119 m).

THE SOUTH COAST AND THE AEGEAN

The south coast of Turkey is rich in Hellenic, Byzantine, Armenian and
Crusader remains as well as many fine Turkish buildings. It is for this

that I feel Turkey is worth a separate trip. You can go along the coast where the Hellenic tours go and get to the place of interest before the crush and to the little places where all is green and silent under the round blue-silver of olive groves, where the large buses cannot reach. To get there it is possible to drive south from a turning between Erzerum and Erzinçan through Elazig, Malatya, Adana and Mersin. This road due south is very beautiful, but the surface is rough and as it is against the grain of the country, it is very stiff motoring with some high passes.

Ankara to Tarsus – 285 miles. This is the best route to take south. Going round Ankara on your return journey you pick up the road for Konya, Kayseri and Adana, the 1 (E5), where it leaves the road for Instamboul at the traffic lights you passed on your way in. You go past the race-course, over another crossroads and on again across a clover-leaf fly-over. The road goes across the rather monotonous Anatolian plain and is not particularly exciting. Sixty-seven miles out of the capital a right-hand fork leads to Konya. If you want to visit the home of the whirling dervishes do this as a side trip since the road south from Konya to the coast is appalling.

After Ulukisla, 4,680 ft, about 217 miles from Ankara, you enter the Taurus Mountains and pass through the gorge of the Cilician Gates, making for Adana till you reach the junction with 6 (E24) seventy-eight miles farther on. A Roman Emperor put up a tablet to commemorate Alexander's forced march through here before the battle of the Issus. It is still there.

At the road junction, turn right and three kilometres farther on you come to Tarsus, the birthplace of St Paul.

Tarsus to Korikos – 55 miles. There is a very good Mocamp at Korikos (Corycus), just opposite the island castle of Kis Kalesi. From here you can explore all along the coast. Erdemli, forty miles out of Tarsus is an excellent place for shopping – particularly fish, olives and fruit.

Korikos to Antalya – 270 miles. This is an extraordinarily lovely road. It winds up and down through Mediterranean pines and is seldom out of sight of the sea. There are ruins all the way and flowers too in this botanist's paradise. They make a lovely foreground to vast hills and mountains of bare rock, not dull but beautiful in soft green, pink and purple tints. However, the road is narrow and dangerous in places, so be careful.

There is a splendid castle on Roman foundations at Anamur a hundred miles from Korikos and a good mocamp just beyond Alanya, seventy miles on. Between Alanya and Antalya you come to one of the areas richest in archaelogical ruins. The signposts to these are in dull ochre yellow. I would particularly mention Side, Aspendos and Perge.

Antalya to Dinar – 113 miles. Here you leave the coast and go inland for Izmir (Smyrna), heading north at first. I believe that a road is being built right round the coast where there has so far never been one. You cross two passes, the Cubuk Bogazi, 2,375 ft and the Beli, 4,000 ft and at Dinar swing west.

Dinar to Seljuk (Akincilar) – 172 miles. Sixty miles out you come to the road junction for Pamukkale and Hieropolis, two of Turkey's greatest sights. The first is a splendid amphitheatre of white cliffs, petrified lime with warm springs, and the latter an ancient ruined Roman town.

After Denizli you follow the Meander River through plains of vines, olives and bittersweet-smelling figs. The ruins at Nyssa, fifty-eight miles out, are of the private kind. A small road leads you up into the hills, where you will find a theatre and forum – a place of truly perfect peace, undisturbed and untenanted, a ruin all to yourself shared only with flowers and the lazy hum of bees.

Seljuk southwards. At Seljuk you swing south for Ephesus (which needs no description) and all the small towns and harbours that lie along the coast. There are good camps the whole way along and in the summer the area is full of tourists. Alternatively you can turn back towards the Dardanelles and Europe.

Ephesus to Canakkale – 242 miles. The road is quite good and goes round Izmir after passing through the Torbali River gorge. There are many places you can visit on the way up the coast as far as Troy, but the one that I most remember is Bergama or Pergamum; a hundred and ten miles out from Ephesus a road forks right to this town, four miles away. Psychological methods are not new; they were practiced here by the Aesculapian priests. They believed in sleep and making their patients take exercise and probably hallucinating drugs. At their temples on the hill high above the town the patients filed down into a round house and along its underground passages while priests adopting resonant, godlike voices gave them pep talks or hoarsely whispered truths down stone funnels slanted to the patients' ears. Everybody felt a lot better and the clinic must have done well.

Back on the main road you leave the coastal lowlands near Edremit, a hundred and seventy-five miles out, and climb over the pine-clad shoulders of the hills to drop again to the plains of Troy (Truva). The junction for Troy is two hundred and forty miles out and the site is three or four miles off the main road. It does not have a great deal to reveal, but nothing could spoil for us the romance of actually standing where Hector and Achilles fought and the wooden horse was dragged into the walls of Troy. Murmuring, 'Timeo Danaos et dona ferentes,' we sped on our way to Canakkale and the ferryboat.

This ferry runs about once every hour and a half and is as efficient as its grander confrères at Istamboul. We found we had to wait for it for some time, but we also found that we were waiting opposite a shop that sold the most delicious Turkish Delight – both the plain kind and that stuffed with nuts, honey and other trifles. We bought a couple of boxes for the family, but they never reached England. We ate them up ourselves, quite unable to resist them.

The ferry duly deposited us at Ecebat after a quiet and leisurely crossing over those straits that have seen so many armies, not least those of the Gallipoli Campaign of the first World War.

Ecebat to Keşan – 75 miles. The road to Keşan where you rejoin the outward route from Alexandropolis to Istamboul is uneventful, except for Turkish trucks and narrow places. There are plenty of places to stop for the night by the sea after leaving Ecebat.

BURSA

This town in the centre of the peach-growing area was the first capital of the Ottoman Turks and has some tiled mosques and mausoleums of extraordinary beauty. Turkish skills in tilework were first perfected here. The thermal baths date from Roman times and are still in everyday use. Bursa can be approached from Canakkale on the route out of Turkey, described above, from Izmir, or from Ankara. Your journey can then be continued towards Istamboul, either by ferry across the Sea of Marmora or by going round its southern shore to rejoin your outward route at Izmit.

Canakkale to Bursa – 193 miles. The road skirts the Sea of Marmora as far as Sevketiye and then runs across a fertile plain to the ancient capital.

Izmir to Bursa – 220 miles. The road goes inland via Manisa and Balikesir until it eventually joins the road from Canakkale.

Ankara to Bursa – 242 miles. This route runs through Eskisehir (145 miles from Ankara). It is a fairly fast road across the undulating Anatolian plain. After Eskisehir it rises and falls until the final descent to Bursa which is only 820 ft above sea level.

Bursa to Istamboul – 152 miles by Izmit: 62 miles by road if you use the ferry. The road winds up to Gemlik (1,300 ft) and continues through hilly country till you drop to the Gulf of Izmit near Yalova (47 m.) Here you can catch the ferry for Kartal, every two hours, and rejoin your outward route fifteen miles from Istamboul. Otherwise continue on eastwards rounds the gulf to Izmit and rejoin your route fifty-nine miles short of Istamboul.

This leisurely return will have been far longer than your outward journey, but I have found from experience that making detours such as these does ease the pang of parting from India.

RECIPES

The following recipes are largely Indian ones adapted to camp life. They form a kind of basic diet and can be varied indefinitely.

BREADS
Utensils. Can all be bought cheaply in any bazaar. They are:
Parath – a flat round dish with sloping sides for mixing dough.
Small board and rolling pin.
Tawa – a domed disk of heavy iron for cooking chapattis. It works best on a slow fire. Alternatively use a heavy frying pan.
Puri Dish – a round bottomed aluminium bowl with handles for deep frying.

Chapattis
Ingredients: 1 lb flour (wholemeal or ātta – Indian wholemeal), salt, water, and a little cooking oil.
Method: Mix salt with flour in the parath and make a stiff dough with water. Kneed powerfully and stand for half an hour covered. Make small balls of the mixture and roll out into thin flat cakes. Cook on lightly greased domed side of tawa, previously heated or in frying pan lightly oiled. Turn the cake as soon as it is heated. When thoroughly heated on both sides, put over a red fire or grill to cook through. Eat hot.

Puris
Ingredients: 3 mugs wholemeal flour and 1 of plain white, salt, water and cooking oil.
Method: Mix flours and salt and rub in 1½ tablespoons oil, as for pastry. Make a stiff dough with water, kneeding well. Cover and stand for ½ hour. Then rub in a little more oil and make cakes as for chapattis. Fill puri dish two-thirds full of oil and heat till a clear smoke rises. Drop the cakes in lightly one at a time. Each should rise and inflate. Turn and brown on other side. Drain well. Can be eaten with anything and will keep for three days.

Prathas

Ingredients: 1 lb wholemeal or ātta, butter, salt.

Method: Make a dough as for chapattis and stand for half an hour. Roll out cakes, put a lump of butter or Dhalda (vegetable fat) in the middle, fold in half and fry in a little oil. You can put vegetables, etc. in with fat before folding.

DHAL (Lentils)

Best cooked in a pressure cooker. Follow the recipe in instruction book (see Chapter 11) using *half* the quantity of liquid only. Flavour with curry powder, sliced onions and salt and produce a firm paste when cool, decorated with thin sliced onions fried black and hard. An excellent source of protein.

RICE

Uncle Ben is easiest to cook. Indian rice must be picked over for foreign bodies and carefully and lavishly washed. Put rice in saucepan with double the quantity of cold water and some salt. Bring to boil in open saucepan, cover and simmer slowly until water is absorbed and rice soft. Turn up the heat for a minute and then put rice into a large fine strainer. Stand this over pan of boiling water for five minutes, covered.

Pilao

Ingredients: Stage 1 – 1½ to 2 kilos meat or chicken, 1 oz coriander (dhuniya) seeds, 1 oz fennel, 1 oz sliced garlic, 1 oz fresh ginger sliced, 1 small onion. Stage 2 – 2 cups rice, 1 cup yoghourt (dhai), 1 oz cumin (zira) seeds, cloves, white and black cardamom, peppercorns, salt, cinnamon stick, saffron, 2 handfuls sultanas, 1 handful prunes, 1 large onion sliced. Garnishing – Onions, sliced and fried black, fried nuts, slices of hard boiled egg.

Method: Put ingredients of stage 1 into pressure cooker together with 1½ pints water and some salt. Cook at 15 lbs pressure for 20 minutes and cool at room temperature. Remove meat and cut up. Remove excess fat from stock and strain. Stage 2 – Wash rice as above and soak some strands of saffron in boiling water. Fry onion in 2 tablespoons of oil till golden brown and add spices in quantities to taste using only seeds of black cardamom. I use 1 doz cloves, 6 white cardamom, 6 peppercorns, 2 sticks cinnamon, 12 strands saffron. Add dahi and 3 cups stock (4 cups if dahi unobtainable). Cook for a little and add meat, rice, sultanas and prunes together with salt and the cumin rubbed through your hands. Cover closely and cook very slowly. When moisture all absorbed, add saffron and its water. Turn on large dish (use your parath!) and garnish. Rice grains should be fairly dry and separate.

CURRIES
Potato

Ingredients: 2 lb potatoes sliced, 2 or 3 teaspoons curry powder, tomato purée, stock or stock cube and water, 2 cloves of garlic, and 2 large onions, salt and cooking oil.

Method: Slice onions coarsely and fry till golden in 2 tablespoons of cooking oil. Make a paste, rather liquid, with water, curry powder and salt. Crush garlic in a little liquid and add to paste. When onions are ready pour in paste and cook hard until mixture begins to separate, then add potatoes and tomato purée. Cook for 2 minutes and add a little stock. Cover and cook quite fast until potatoes are soft and curry nearly dry.

Other Vegetables: Same recipe, but perhaps a little more liquid.

Meat – Same method, but definitely more liquid. Best done in pressure cooker.

GLOSSARY OF USEFUL PHRASES AND GREETINGS

I am very loath to make a list of phrases simply because English phonetics approximate only to the sounds you need. I will give you enough to show you are trying to be polite and to enable you to obtain the basic staff of life for yourself and your vehicle. Beyond this you should point to items and get the names repeated until you can pronounce them properly. This will lead to much laughter and friendliness so I purposely leave you in the lurch here. It is more important to pronounce words well than to be grammatical. Unless a word is properly pronounced it will be difficult to make people understand and the Turks won't even try.

TURKISH

Good morning	Gûnaydīn
Good night	Gechelu hayû olsūn
Hallo	Murhabba (not to ladies or elders)
Good-bye	Allaha ismārladik (by person leaving). It means roughly 'Commit me to God'
Good-bye	Güle Güle (by person seeing off). It means Go laughingly or Good-bye and Good Luck.
Please	Lūtfĕn
Thank you	Tĕshĕkūr ĕdĕrĭm
Welcome (by host)	Khush geldiniz
Reply	Khush bŏldūhr
Don't mention it	Beer shāy dāyîl
On being introduced	Mūsheriff eldūm (I have been honoured)
Reply	Sheriff bănă ait (The honour is mine)
Petrol	Benzīn
Diesel	Diezĕl or Motorīn
Oil	Yagi
Water	Sū
Bread	Ekmek
Insurance	Sigorta

PERSIAN (Use in Iran and Afghanistan except the South)

How do you do	Salāam āleikum
Reply	Wāleikum es salāam
Good-bye	Khudār Hāfiz
Reply	Khudār-Hāfiz-i-Shuma
Petrol	Benzin
Diesel	Naftgaz
Oil	Raughan
Water	Ab
Bread	Nan
Insurance	Bime (pronounced Bee-may)

PUSHTU (Use in South Afghanistan and N.W.F.P. of Pakistan)

The greetings below are always accompanied by a handshake

How do you do	Stere mā she (May you not be tired)
Reply	Te stere mā she (May you also not be tired)
More common reply	Quar mā she (May you not become poor)
You are welcome	Pa ker rāgle
Good-bye	Per makha de kha (literally, Good in your face). Said by person seeing off
Good-bye	Ămin tā sara (Peace be with you). Said by person going
Thank you	Shukr or shukr de or sta dehr mehrabani
Don't mention it	Hïs shāy dāyïl
Petrol	Benzin
Diesel	Diesel or Naft gaz
Oil	Tel. Specify type; da engine tel, da gearbox tel, da differential tel, etc.
Water	Obo
Bread	Nān
Insurance	Use English

URDU/HINDI (In Pakistan and N. India)

How do you do	Salaam – chiefly in Pakistan. Namaste – for Hindus. Usually accompanied by the hands together in an attitude of prayer. No Indian can tell you clearly what it means – it is just a greeting
Good-bye	As above
Petrol	Benzin
Diesel	Diesel
Oil	Tel

Water	Pāni
Bread	Roti or Dubbar Roti for leavened bread
Insurance	Use English
Please	Mehr bahni
Thank you	Shukriya

From Bombay southwards use English. People generally refuse to understand Hindi. The languages of the extreme south, i.e. Telegu, Tamil and Malayalam are very tongue-twisting and it is not necessary to speak them. English is widespread.

BOOKS FOR FURTHER READING

Of the standard series of guides for the countries covered by this book, Nagel has the merit of being published in three languages – French, German and English – and Fodor, while not so strong in other directions, is good on motoring. Cape have a volume on Turkey in their Traveller's Guide series. The leading guide for the Indian subcontinent is the Murray *Handbook to India, Pakistan, Bangladesh and Sri Lanka*, now in its twenty-second edition.

Turkey
David Hotham, *The Turks*, John Murray 1972
Peter Mayne, *Istanbul*, J. M. Dent 1967
Freya Stark, *Ionia*, John Murray 1954
Freya Stark, *The Lycian Shore*, John Murray 1956
Freya Stark, *Alexander's Path*, John Murray 1958
Freya Stark, *Rome on The Euphrates*, John Murray 1966

Iran
A. Cecil Edwards, *The Persian Carpet*, Duckworth 1976
Sir Roger Stevens, *Land of the Great Sophy*, Methuen 1971
Philip Ward, *Touring Iran*, Faber 1971

Afghanistan
Peter Levi, *The Light Garden of the Angel King*, Collins 1972
Freya Stark, *The Minaret of Djam*, John Murray 1970

India and Pakistan
John Keay, *Into India*, John Murray 1973, paperback 1975
Arthur Swinson, *North-West Frontier*, Corgi Books 1969
Romila Thapar, *A History of India* vol I, Penguin Books 1970
Percival Spear, *A History of India* vol II, Penguin Books 1970.

SOME CAMPS IN ASIA

TURKEY
Ankara – Suzuzkoy, B.P. Mocamp on road to Istamboul
Alanya – B.P. Mocamp on road to Antalya
Edirne – B.P. Mocamp on road to Istamboul
Erzerum – B.P. Parking site, no facilities, on Asian Highway
Ipsala – B.P. Mocamp on main road near border
Istamboul (Kartal Tepe) – B.P. Mocamp on main road to city; Shell Mocamp on main road to city
Kusudasi – B.P. Mocamp for Ephesus, etc.
Nevsehir – B.P. Mocamp on road to Göreme
Silifke – B.P. Mocamp on coast road at Kizkalesi
Sivas – B.P. Parking site, no facilities, on road into Sivas
Trabzon – B.P. Mocamp at Wakfikebir, 30 miles along coast from Trabzon

Besides these there are numerous camps belonging to the Oil Companies and private owners along the Sea of Marmora, the Aegean and Mediterranean coasts and the Black Sea, built chiefly to cater for tourists from Germany.

IRAN
Isfahan – Shahkooh, S. of Isfahan-Shahkooh road
Mashhad – Off Asian Highway by-pass
Tabriz – S.E. of city off Asian Highway
Teheran – Gol-e-Sahra, on Saveh/Isfahan road
Shiraz – On the airport road

You can stop the night almost anywhere in Iran. The officially listed camps are so difficult to find that it is better to make your own arrangements, except for those noted above.

OTHER COUNTRIES
See relevant Chapters.

Index

Index